Praise for *Indoctrination U.*

"Much has been written about the politicization of college education by selfish radicals who preach rather than teach. This book describes the only sustained national effort to correct the problem. Horowitz gives us a careful, analytical account of key episodes in the campaign for an Academic Bill of Rights that will surprise many whose impression has been formed by distorted and deceitful accounts from its opponents. Though Horowitz's campaign is solidly based on venerable policy statements of the American Association of University Professors, today's radicalized AAUP leadership has bitterly attacked the Academic Bill of Rights, thereby disowning the AAUP's own core principles. Everyone who cares about a genuinely liberal college education—regardless of political perspective—will be grateful for David Horowitz's tireless, relentless, and above all well-judged efforts to rescue it from the intellectual trivialization and monotony of radical politics. Nobody else has done so much or been so effective."

> **—John M. Ellis,** Professor Emeritus of German literature, University of California at Santa Cruz; Founding Secretary of the Association of Literary Scholars and Critics; and President of the California Association of Scholars

"Horowitz's modus operandi has been to expose some of the academy's zaniest enclaves. He has compiled a veritable encyclopedia of anecdotes revealing betrayal upon betrayal of the notion of the disinterested, scholarly classroom setting. Many of these are retold in this well-sourced book, which reads as a blend of political tract and personal memoir."

> **—Travis Kavulla,** Gates Scholar in African history, Cambridge University; and former associate editor of *National Review*

INDOCTRINATION U.

The Left's War Against
Academic Freedom

DAVID HOROWITZ

ENCOUNTER BOOKS
NEW YORK · LONDON

Paperback edition published in 2009 by Encounter Books,
an activity of Encounter for Culture and Education, Inc.,
a nonprofit, tax exempt corporation.
Encounter Books website address: www.encounterbooks.com

Manufactured in the United States and printed on
acid-free paper. The paper used in this publication meets
the minimum requirements of ANSI/NISO Z39.48–1992
(R 1997) (*Permanence of Paper*).

Paperback edition ISBN: 978-1-594032-37-0

The Library of Congress has Cataloged the Hardcover Edition as Follows:

Horowitz, David, 1939-
    Indoctrination U.: The Left's War Against Academic Freedom / by
David Horowitz.
    p.   cm.
    ISBN 1-59403-190-8
    1.   Academic freedom—United States.   2.   Education, Higher—
Political aspects—United States.   I.   Title.
LC72.2.H67   2007
378.1'213—dc22

                                                    2006028688

10 9 8 7 6 5 4 3 2 1

To April
Who provides me with the life
that makes the work possible.

The function of the university is to seek and to transmit knowledge and to train students in the processes whereby truth is to be made known. To convert, or to make converts, is alien and hostile to this dispassionate duty. Where it becomes necessary in performing this function of a university, to consider political, social, or sectarian movements, they are dissected and examined, not taught, and the conclusion left, with no tipping of the scales, to the logic of the facts. . . . Essentially the freedom of a university is the freedom of competent persons in the classroom. In order to protect this freedom, the University assumed the right to prevent exploitation of its prestige by unqualified persons or by those who would use it as a platform for propaganda.

> —Rule APM 0-10, University of California,
> Berkeley, Academic Personnel Manual.
> Inserted by UC President Robert Gordon
> Sproul, 1934. Removed by a 43–3 vote of the
> UC Academic Senate, July 30, 2003.

Academic freedom is the freedom of academics to study anything they like; the freedom, that is, to subject any body of material, however unpromising it might seem, to academic interrogation and analysis. . . . Any idea can be brought into the classroom if the point is to inquire into its structure, history, influence and so forth. But no idea belongs in the classroom if the point of introducing it is to recruit your students for the political agenda it may be thought to imply.

> —Professor Stanley Fish,
> *New York Times,* July 23, 2006

Contents

Preface to the
Paperback Edition

I had three goals in writing this book. The first was to describe the campaign for an Academic Bill of Rights I launched in the fall of 2003; the second was to provide case studies of the abuses the Academic Bill of Rights was designed to correct; the third was to document the bare-knuckle tactics of the opponents of the bill, who have conducted themselves in a manner more appropriate to a political brawl than to a discussion of academic issues.

From its inception, the proposal for an Academic Bill of Rights inspired fierce controversy. A recently published book, *The Academic Bill of Rights Debate,* describes its impact: "Few academic topics have created such a furor in so short a time. . . . By November of 2006, it had already generated 74 articles in major newspapers, at least 143 articles in all newspapers nationwide, 54 television and radio broadcasts, 47 newswire articles, 20 articles in *The Chronicle of Higher Education,* 73 articles in *Inside-HigherEd.com,* dozens of articles in major magazines, and some 154,000 hits in the obligatory Google search."[1]

Edited by a professor of education at the University of Akron, *The Academic Bill of Rights Debate* sets out to present the controversy in an academic manner but instead joins it. Every contributor to the volume but one manifests extreme hostility to the reform which is a liberal measure based on long-standing academic tradition. (The exception is the author of the Academic Bill of Rights.) The flavor of some of the attacks is reflected in a contribution by Princeton professor Joan Wallach Scott who describes the reform in these words: "It recalls the kind of government intervention in the academy practiced by totalitarian governments (historical examples are Japan, Nazi Germany, China, Fascist Italy and the Soviet Union) who seek to control thought rather than permit a free marketplace of ideas."[2] In point of fact, the Academic Bill of Rights calls for *no* government intervention in the academy and is an effort to *protect* students from thought control. It was specifically designed to thwart faculty attempts to indoctrinate students by presenting professorial opinion as scientific fact and by failing to assign texts critical of faculty orthodoxy.

Even the editor of *The Academic Bill of Rights Debate* joins the assault. Instead of providing an introduction summarizing the discussion in a dispassionate manner, the editor indulges in tendentious attacks on the Academic Bill of Rights and its author. Although the Academic Bill of Rights is explicitly designed to articulate long-established principles of academic freedom, the editor introduces his text with the following statement: "...The Academic Bill of Rights is a recent and controversial attack on traditional notions of academic freedom..." which is the very opposite of the truth.[3]

Another text largely devoted to attacking the academic freedom campaign has been written by John K. Wilson, publisher of the webzine *Illinois Academe* and long associated with the academic left. According to Wilson, "The Academic Bill of Rights is the story of how David Horowitz, pretending to stand up for 'student rights' and moral conduct by professors, led a crusade to have legislators force every college in the country to adopt the most coercive system of grievance procedures and investigations of liberal professors ever proposed in America."[4]

This statement is false on every account. Despite Wilson's claim, the "Academic Bill of Rights" contains *no* provision for grievance machinery. In crafting my proposals for academic reform I have been careful to respect the independence of academic institutions. I have consequently regarded the problem of enforcement better left to university faculty and administrators to devise. I have not proposed a single piece of legislation to "force" colleges to adopt *any* reforms, and have never proposed legislation to create academic grievance procedures. Nor have I ever called for "investigations of liberal professors." In fact, I have opposed making the point of view of professors a subject for remedial measures. I have said publicly (and repeatedly) that "bias" is not an issue, that every individual has a "bias" and professors have a right to express theirs in their classrooms so long as they do so in a professional manner, and in accordance with the principles of academic freedom. What faculty may not do is to *impose* their bias on students through coercive grading, or by failing to provide them with critical reading materials, or by presenting their personal prejudices as established wisdom.

The unprincipled campaign against the Academic Bill of Rights has been conducted almost exclusively by two left-wing teacher organizations—the American Association of University Professors and the American Federation of Teachers. These organizations represent less than 10% of all faculty at institutions of higher learning but they are able to present themselves as the voice of the faculty because the vast majority of academics have chosen to maintain a discreet silence on these matters, perhaps to avoid becoming targets of similar unprincipled attacks.

The influence of this aggressive political minority should not be underestimated. In a situation where there is widespread misrepresentation of the positions in an argument, it is difficult for more disinterested parties to get the facts straight. This problem is evident in a third book to appear since the publication of *Indoctrination U* that makes the Academic Bill of Rights a focus of concern. *Closed Minds? Politics and Ideology in American Universities* is a publication of the Brookings Institution, and is the only one of these three texts, which attempts to provide a dispassionate view of these issues.[5] Written by three academics, including a former university president, *Closed Minds* is promoted by a blurb that praises its "solid empirical research, historical breadth and sober impartiality."

While a far cry from the polemical caricatures of the other titles, the description of the academic freedom campaign in *Closed Minds,* is often untrustworthy: "[Horowitz's] proposals included funding for legislative 'watchdog' staffs, investigating student complaints of classroom bias, and imposing annual reporting requirements on public colleges and universities."[6] This statement is wrong on two of three items mentioned. I have never supported a legislative watchdog staff or an annual reporting requirement.[7] Both of these have been proposed in "diversity" legislation by the American Council of Trustees and Alumni, which I have not supported.

A section of *Closed Minds* focuses on a project that I did put my efforts behind. Unfortunately, it misrepresents it as well. The Pennsylvania Hearings on Academic Freedom held in 2005 and 2006 The Pennsylvania hearings led to the creation at Penn State and Temple University of the first academic freedom provisions for students anywhere in the United States. These events are discussed in *Indoctrination U* but the authors of Closed Minds have overlooked them and failed to understand what they achieved.[8] As a direct result of the hearings, Penn State and Temple also created the first (and only) grievance machinery to be provided by American universities to handle student complaints related to academic freedom.[9]

The account of the Pennsylvania hearings provided in *Closed Minds* follows closely the script of the teacher unions and their legislative allies, and consequently fails to mention either of these singular achievements. Its inaccuracies begin with a false account of the origins of the Committee on Academic Freedom that legislators created to hold the hearings. According to *Closed Minds* "the precipitating event" that led to the creation of the Committee was an erroneous claim that originated with me, namely that Michael Moore's film *Farenheit 9/11* was shown in a Penn State biology class prior to the 2004 presidential election. Both statements are used by the authors to discredit the hearings. Following the teacher union script, they conclude that the hearings were a "solution" in search of a problem that didn't exist.

But, as the public record shows, the allegations on which this script is based are false. The event that actually inspired

Representative Gibson Armstrong to sponsor the legislation creating the Pennsylvania Committee had nothing to do with a showing of *Farenheit 9/11* in a biology class. The actual origins of this legislation were reported in a *New York Times* article "Professors' Politics Draw Lawmakers Into the Fray," which appeared on December 25, 2005, shortly after the hearings began. The article, written by reporter, Michael Janofsky, identified the actual "precipitating event" as a Republican Party picnic. Armstrong was approached by one of his constituents, an Iraq War veteran named Jennie Mae Brown, who complained that she had been subjected to rants on the Iraq War by her physics professor at a Penn State.[10] This episode inspired Armstrong to begin drafting legislation and to consult me as an academic reformer for advice on how to proceed. I have re-told this story twice for publication—in an op-ed in the *Los Angeles Times* a month after the Janofsky article appeared, and also in the text of *Indoctrination U,* so there is little excuse for the three authors of *Closed Minds* who got this wrong.[11]

Not only is *Closed Minds* in error in stating that a claim about *Farenheit 9/11* provided the inspiration for Armstrong's legislation, it is wrong in claiming that the charge originated with me. It did not. The claim about *Farenheit 9/11* was made by a member of Representative Armstrong's staff and I heard it from him. I then casually referred to it on a couple of occasions as one of many other classroom examples of why such hearings were needed. At the same time, I provided scores of other cases of abusive faculty behavior—all ignored by the Democratic legislators, the teacher unions, and the authors of *Closed Minds.* Moreover, months before the Pennsylvania hearings began, a biology professor at Penn State protested that the charge was groundless and asked Armstrong to provide a source for the charge. When members of Armstrong's staff could not substantiate the claim, I never referred to it again.

Notwithstanding these facts, the authors of *Closed Minds* make the *Farenheit 9/11* episode—which was a trivial matter and wholly incidental to the Pennsylvania reform effort—the focus of five pages of their book, almost half the space they allot to their entire discussion of the hearings.[12] They do so not because this claim was important either to the testimony before the Pennsylvania Committee or to the reform effort itself, but because it was the centerpiece of the attacks on the reform effort by the teacher unions, and by the Democratic opponents of reform who sat on the Committee. These attacks were led by Representative Lawrence Curry, who was both the co-chair of the Committee and a leader of the opposition to its hearings. Curry had voted against the legislation that created the Committee and authorized the hearings and he attacked the proceedings throughout. Nor did he confine his opposition to the Committee chambers and the hearing room. Curry was the keynote speaker at two protest rallies organized by the teacher unions, at which the then ongoing hearings were denounced as a "McCarthy witch-hunt."[13] None of these facts is mentioned by the authors of *Closed Minds*.

I was the last witness to testify at the hearing sessions held at Temple University on January 9 and 10, 2005.[14] In my testimony I introduced the signed statement of a pro-life student at Penn State named Kelly Keelan.[15] Keelan described a Women's Studies class she had taken in which her professor instructed students that women should be "proud" of their abortions and then made them all stand and chant "abortion, abortion." Keelan testified that she was reduced to tears by this demonstration because she felt there was no place for her in the class. Nor did such a demonstration have anything to do with the academic study of women. This was precisely the kind of abuse the Academic Bill of Rights was designed to prevent. Curry showed no interest in Keelan's complaint or in the testimony of student Logan Fisher, who also provided examples of faculty abuse. Nor did any of the Democratic legislators (or the authors of *Closed Minds*) show any concern about the students who filed complaints with Representative Armstrong but asked that their names be withheld out of fear of reprisal. Instead, in order to distract attention from these abuses and to create the impression that they did not exist, in the last minutes of the hearing session Curry and one of his colleagues focused their attention on the erroneous claim about Michael Moore's *Farenheit 9/11,* which had been no part of my testimony or that of any other proponent of academic reform during the ten hours of hearings.

Curry wanted to know if I had or would "retract" the statement about the Moore film. I pointed out that the claim did not originate with me and was no part of my testimony and was, in any case, irrelevant to the proceedings. But Curry and a fellow Democrat on the Committee persisted in pressing me to say whether I had "retracted" the statement. This was a "when-did-you-stop-beating-your-wife?" type of question. If I admitted to retracting it, the presumption would be (and was) that it was material to my case for reform, which it was not. If I refused to answer, and thus failed to concede that it was false, I would be guilty of making up stories to establish the need for reform. Curry's intent in hectoring me over the issue was to stigmatize me for the benefit of a hostile education media covering the hearings, who would be sure to repeat the charge.

Predictably the headline for the lead story appearing the next day in *InsideHigherEd.com,* an online journal which never veered far from the teacher-union talking points, was "Retractions From Horowitz." In the story that followed, my testimony and that of other witnesses supporting the need for an Academic Bill of Rights was ignored. Instead the author, editor Scott Jaschik, focused relentlessly on the "retraction." In their own version of what transpired, the authors of *Closed Minds* elevate this political sideshow into a defining moment of the proceedings. This fiction is made plausible by their false claim that the *Farenheit 9/11* matter was the "precipitating event" that led to the creation of the academic freedom hearings.

In drawing their own lessons from the hearings, the authors of *Closed Minds* follow the conclusions of the Committee's final report. But what the authors do not mention is that this document was the product of an eleventh-hour coup by the

Democratic minority, which led to an evisceration of the original report and a rewriting of its recommendations. The coup was the work of a coalition of Committee members opposed to reform and, in fact, to the hearings themselves. The coalition included two Republicans who had defected from the Committee majority after Democrats won control of the Pennsylvania House in an election that occurred while the hearings were in session. This emboldened the Democratic minority to forge an alliance with Republicans who had opposed the hearings from the outset.[16] The anti-reform coalition was able to block a vote of the Republican caucus which would have ratified the original report a week before the deadline, and then, on the very eve of the deadline, the coalition gutted the report and rewrote its conclusions.[17]

The original report had contained a lengthy "Summary of Testimony," which reviewed the ten months of hearings and reported their findings.[18] On the basis of the summarized evidence, this section of the original report concluded that no academic freedom protections for Pennsylvania students were in place when the Committee began its hearings. The academic freedom provisions that did exist were to be found only in employee handbooks and teacher-union contracts and clearly referred to rights of faculty not students. The original report therefore recommended that "*student-specific* academic freedom rights" be adopted: "Public institutions of higher learning within the Commonwealth should review existing academic freedom policies and procedures to ensure that a student-specific academic freedom policy, which ensures student rights and a detailed grievance procedure are readily available."[19]

Because the coup took place the evening before the deadline for submitting the report, there was no time to write a new one. The coup team simply gutted the actual report, taking out the entire "Summary of Testimony" and review of findings. They then rewrote the Committee recommendations, although now there was no substantiating material in the report to back up its conclusions. In other words, the "report" was no longer really a report on the proceedings; it was just an assertion of the opinions of the new majority.

In rewriting the report's conclusions, the new majority dropped the recommendation that universities adopt "student-specific academic freedom policies." Instead, the new version concluded that "academic freedom violations were rare," something the Committee did not investigate, and that it was impossible for the Committee—or anyone else—to know, since there were no existing academic freedom provisions for students at Pennsylvania's public universities and no grievance procedures available to students to file academic freedom complaints should they so desire.[20]

That creating student-specific rights was both necessary and actually a non-partisan issue was confirmed while the hearings were in session when the Penn State faculty passed a resolution which for the first time applied Penn State's existing academic freedom regulation to students. (Until then, it had been only available in the Penn State Employee Handbook.)[21]

In the fall of 2008, a Penn State student named Abigail Beardsley attempted to avail herself the newly created grievance machinery. Beardsley had enrolled in a French class described in the college catalogue as a course in the French language—French vocabulary and syntax. But during one of the classroom sessions, the professor showed his students a portion of Michael Moore's film *Sicko*. Like Moore's other "documentaries," *Sicko* is a political propaganda film, which makes a case for socialized medicine and Fidel Castro's police state. Abigail Beardsley regarded its showing as a violation of Penn State's new student academic freedom policy. Here is an excerpt from her complaint:

> According to the syllabus for French 112, the course objective is to develop students' skills in reading, writing and speaking the French language. The catalogue description defines the course goal as not only that the student should "acquire new knowledge of the French language, but ...also build upon what you have already learned as a student of French. The focus of the course is on real-life language

use, the integrations of language and culture, and the development
of the four skills: listening, speaking, reading, and writing.

The clarity of these objectives is admirable. But during the spring
semester of 2008, Nate Sebold, the instructor for Section 1 of French
112 took valuable class time to show the controversial Michael Moore
propaganda film *Sicko,* which is an attack on the free market health
care system in the United States and an endorsement of socialized
medicine in England, Canada, France and Communist Cuba. The
section of Moore's film praising France's socialized health care system was shown to the class on March 19th. No critical evaluations
of the film or contrary views of socialized medicine were provided
by the instructor, which would have allowed students to think for
themselves on these controversial matters. Penn State Policy HR64
explicitly requires instructors to "provide [students] access to those
materials which they need if they are to think intelligently." It further instructs professors not to introduce controversial materials that
are irrelevant to the class subject and outside their area of professional expertise. The showing of *Sicko* in French 112 was a clear violation of both these principles and of Policy HR64 and is the
gravamen of my complaint.[22]

Widespread classroom showings of Moore's films *Bowling
for Columbine, Farenheit 9/11,* and *Sicko*—without critical commentary—provide a useful index of the decline of intellectual
standards documented in *Indoctrination U.* These showings are
naked attempts to persuade students of the correctness of the
instructors' personal views and could not occur without the similarly widespread acceptance of political agitation as a suitable
form of classroom instruction.

When Abigail Beardsley filed her complaint, the chairman
of the French Department supported the showing of Moore's
propaganda and rejected her appeal. Without support from other
members of the Penn State faculty Beardsley became discouraged, and decided not to pursue her case. Another Penn State
student, A. J. Fluehr filed a successful complaint, but was also discouraged by the process which dragged over 11 months and pit-
ted him against the department chair and faculty members who
clearly regarded his concerns as frivolous and himself as a

nuisance. Fluehr's complaint was only resolved positively after he submitted it to the college dean.[23]

There are no visible conservatives on the faculty at Penn State and no significant support among liberal faculty for students such as Abigail Beardsley and A. J. Fluehr. The difficulty of filing student complaints in a hostile environment with uncertain repercussions from faculty members was raised at the hearings of the Pennsylvania Committee on Academic Freedom but could not be seriously addressed in the partisan atmosphere. For all intents and purposes, efforts to institute what ought to be a simple policy to protect students continues to be stymied.

These episodes provide a benchmark of the success achieved by the entrenched opponents of academic freedom. As *Indoctrination U.* documents, and as books such as *Closed Minds* demonstrate, the denial that there is even a problem remains a prevailing attitude. In the bitterly contested atmosphere created by the opponents of reform, little progress is likely to be made, and the decline of academic standards will continue. This is unfortunate for both liberal and conservative students alike, and is why *Indoctrination U* was written.

Los Angeles, January, 2009

Preface

During the last twenty years, I have spoken at more than three hundred universities, where I interviewed students and professors about the intellectual climate on their campuses. In the course of these visits I became concerned about the changes that had taken place since I attended college half a century ago. I was particularly troubled by the increasingly intolerant atmosphere of the schools I visited and by the relentless intrusion of political agendas into an academic environment where they did not belong.

As a result, in the fall of 2002 I began an effort to address these problems by reviving doctrines of academic freedom that were an integral part of university governance but had been increasingly abandoned as a practice in recent decades. I had first encountered these doctrines during my undergraduate years at Columbia College, in the McCarthy period, when they provided a bulwark against the turbulence of those troubled times. Their origins could be traced back yet another half century to the Progressive Era, when professors had been forced to defend themselves from the meddling of benefactors who were angered by academic critiques of their business practices. The principles of academic freedom were devised at that time to ensure that scholars could publish the results of their professional research without fear of reprisals from donors and politicians who lacked their academic expertise.

In recent years, by contrast, it is faculty members who have intruded a political agenda into the academic curriculum and have sought to close down intellectual discussion and prevent open-minded inquiries into "sensitive" subjects. Ideas deemed "reactionary" and "politically incorrect" are suppressed through "speech codes" and a collective disapproval that renders them *ver-*

boten. Unlike previous attempts to interfere with disinterested inquiry, the new political assault comes from faculty insiders who regard their scholarship as a partisan activity and the university as a platform from which they hope to change the world.

The radical attempt to turn schools into agencies for social change is a recent development that coincides with the emergence of "political correctness" as the signature feature of a radicalized academic culture. "Political correctness" is a term that describes an orthodoxy or party line, in this case reflecting the agendas of the left. Ideas that oppose left-wing orthodoxy—opposition to racial preferences, belief in innate differences between men and women, or, more recently, support for America's war in Iraq—are regarded as morally unacceptable or simply indecent. The proponents of such ideas are regarded as deviants from the academic norm, to be marginalized and shunned.

In defending their position, faculty radicals are quick to deny that an orthodoxy is something new to the academic world. In their view, a conservative orthodoxy has always governed the educational curriculum. The objection, they contend, is not to the establishment of an orthodoxy as such, but to an orthodoxy that is not conservative. In this view, conservatives are merely defending the status quo ante, objecting to change. As evidence, radicals point to the "consensus" view of American history as an orthodoxy that prevailed in the preceding generation, and has now been overthrown.

This argument is misconceived. It is true that there has always been an American consensus, but only as a common heritage of shared national memories and common civic virtues. Contrary to the radical claim, the consensus view of American history was not one that excluded ideas because they were dissenting. On the contrary, it embraced them as expressions of American pluralism. The consensus view was more like a patriotic accord: a shared appreciation of the wisdom of the American founding and the value of the democratic, multi-ethnic republic the Framers created. The embrace of this legacy represents a unity indispensable to the social cohesion of a nation that is not based on blood and soil, but on a social contract established at its founding—a nation "*conceived in liberty*" and dedicated to propositions that its constituent elements shared.

Within this American consensus there has always been ample room for dissent and for views that are sharply self-critical, even of the American project itself. The American consensus has always embraced a wide-ranging spectrum that includes the disaffected, provided they seek redress of grievances through the democratic process. In other words, this consensus is not an orthodoxy of the political right; it is the social contract of a historically constructed nation and a community, diverse in its origins and plural in its views. The preservation of this diversity and its democracy is the heart of the consensus. The consensus, in short, is the common cultural bond of the democracy of which all Americans are a part: out of many, *one*. It is this bond that is now under assault from radicals who have entrenched themselves in the university culture.[1]

Side by side with this American consensus—and reflecting its values—there has been until recently a common understanding of the function of education in a democracy. This has included respect for intellectual disagreement as the necessary condition for the development of independent minds. In the modern era it embraces the idea that research and teaching are professional disciplines, which observe the scientific method and require intellectual objectivity and restraint; it insists on a perspective that is expert, skeptical and dispassionate; and it respects the uncertainty of human knowledge and the pluralism of views on which a democracy is based. It is consequently a consensus that opposes the imposition of ideological orthodoxies and sectarian agendas in the classroom.

The new political orthodoxies insinuated into our universities by the left are quite different. They do not derive from the traditions of a shared American heritage and culture, but are sectarian attempts to subvert both—by deconstructing the nation's identity and by dividing its communities into warring classes, genders and races—into victims and oppressors. For academic radicals who hope to "change the world," teaching is not a disinterested intellectual inquiry but a form of political combat. The banner of this combat is "social justice," the emblem that signifies to the post-Communist left the triumph of the oppressed over the oppressors.

An academic movement for "social justice" has inserted its radical agenda into the very templates of collegiate institutions and academic programs, and into the curricula of secondary schools as well.[2] Pursuit of this goal both requires and justifies indoctrinating students in the ideas that radicals regard as "transformative" and "progressive." Far from being a consensus that supports the pluralistic community of the American social contract, the political correctness of the left is the orthodoxy of one social faction seeking to impose its agenda on all the others—a new and disturbing development in the educational culture.

This book describes an effort to disarm the political assault on our schools and to revive the values—professionalism, political neutrality and intellectual diversity—that previously constituted their common foundation. The academic freedom campaign was launched in 2003 when I published an "Academic Bill of Rights," designed to restore intellectual diversity and academic standards. The response is already powerful enough to have acquired a life of its own. In the spring of 2006, the student body at Princeton University passed a "Student Bill of Rights" based on the principles I had proposed, but without any direct intervention by myself or the organization I had created, Students for Academic Freedom. The Princeton bill was the creation of the Princeton students themselves. The same self-propelled efforts can be seen in new movements for academic freedom on more than 150 campuses across the nation.[3]

These campaigns reflect a widespread desire among college students and the general public to restore intellectual pluralism and organizational neutrality to academic institutions, and to protect their scholarly mission. They represent a revulsion against the corruption of the classroom by academics who willfully confuse education with activism and who seek to suppress opposing viewpoints in the name of progressive agendas.[4]

Because the attacks on the academic freedom campaign have focused to a great extent on me as the individual responsible, the narrative that follows necessarily deals with personal experiences.★ The political left which has orchestrated these attacks has a long history of conducting its campaigns through ad hominem charges. It is not for nothing that the word "purge," for example, is a left-wing coinage, or that every purge has featured the slander of its individual targets. The political purge is a purification ritual and its roots can be traced to the fact that radical politics is essentially a religious vocation.

This religious character is determined by the fact that its adherents conceive their projects as "revolutionary" or "transformative"—secular terms for what in effect would be a religious "redemption," albeit an earthly one. Looked at from this vantage, the radical goal is a secular redemption of society from its vale of "oppression." The redemption is accomplished by creating a world without "racism," "sexism" or "classism," the current term of art for which is "social justice"—a secular version of heaven on earth.

The extravagant goal of redeeming humanity justifies uncompromising means. Social redeemers regard themselves as an "army of the saints," and their opponents as the party of sinners. They do not view their conservative opponents as supporters of alternative means for improving the lot of women, minorities and the poor, but as enemies of women, minorities and the poor. Progressive agendas cannot be opposed, therefore, on grounds

---

★These attacks have been so numerous and so reckless that I have not attempted to respond to each and every accusation in this book. While I have described and analyzed many here, other responses can be found in replies to critics at: http://www.frontpagemag.com/Content/read.asp?ID=108; and www.studentsforacademicfreedom.org.

that are principled or practical or compassionate. Opponents of "progressives" are *defined* as "reactionaries"—advocates of racism and sexism, practitioners of "McCarthyism," and other incarnations of social evil.

Consequently, to be demonized by "progressives," as in fact I have been as a result of my efforts in behalf of academic freedom, is not a personal matter, but an ineluctable consequence of opposing their agendas. The anathemas that academic leftists have pronounced on me and the academic freedom campaign have a long and squalid history in the left's battles with previous opponents. The story of the campaign against academic freedom, therefore, can also be read as a study in the methods of the radical project itself.

Los Angeles, August 2006

ONE

Academic Freedom

In the winter of 2002, I drew up an Academic Bill of Rights whose purpose was to promote intellectual diversity on college campuses and restore academic values to university classrooms.[1] Although this bill has since been the object of fervid attacks, it is actually a quintessentially liberal document reflecting values embraced by all American institutions of higher learning throughout the modern era. Its text is based on a famous document called the "Declaration of Principles on Academic Freedom and Academic Tenure,"[2] published in 1915 by the American Association of University Professors. These principles have long since been incorporated into the academic policies of most American research universities.

The 1915 Declaration of Principles proposed two basic rights—one for faculty and the other for students. Professors were guaranteed freedom in their professional research, but they were also warned not to use their classroom authority to indoctrinate their students. In the words of the declaration, a teacher should avoid "taking unfair advantage of the student's immaturity by indoctrinating him with the teacher's own opinions before the student has had an opportunity fairly to examine other opinions upon the matters in question, and before he has sufficient knowledge and ripeness of judgment to be entitled to form any definitive opinion of his own."[3]

While this doctrine has been the foundation of the educational governance of universities for nearly a hundred years, in the last several decades it has been increasingly disregarded by faculty and rarely enforced by administrators. My awareness of this fact led me to believe that a new statement of these principles was required. It also convinced me that a national campaign would be needed to inspire renewed commitment by university administrators to enforce the rules that were meant to ensure the fairness and objectivity of the college classroom.

In 1940 and 1970, the American Association of University Professors issued two subsequent statements amplifying the original Declaration of Principles. Both featured clauses cautioning professors to "be careful not to introduce into their teaching controversial matter which has no relation to their subject."[4] Like the original declaration, these statements were published at a time when the nation was torn by controversies over war and peace. Their goal was to insulate the university from the turbulent passions inspired by the First and Second World Wars and the Vietnam War, whose repercussions could damage the academic enterprise. In designing the Academic Bill of Rights, I was conscious of the fact that I was doing so in the shadow of the terrorist attacks of 9/11 and a new war against radical Islam, and that we were entering these ominous times with the academic freedom protections in a tenuous state.

The hundreds of interviews I conducted with students had made me aware that professors routinely used their classrooms to voice their nonprofessional, and often passionately expressed, opinions on the war in Iraq and other matters that were irrelevant to the subjects they taught and outside their areas of expertise. In the course of these interviews, I rarely encountered a student who had not been subjected to such in-class abuse.[5]

Because student claims to this effect have been regularly— and peremptorily—challenged by faculty opponents of the Academic Bill of Rights, I offer the following two statements by university professors as an indication of how prevalent the use of classrooms for political agendas actually is. These statements appeared on a list-serve managed by the National Endowment for the Humanities for academics whose field is American studies. A question posed to the list by one of the academics was itself revealing of the political, rather than scholarly, mindset of those participating: "How are we in American Studies responding to the war in Iraq (and Afghanistan) as a 'teachable moment'?"

Evelyn Azeeza Alsultany, a professor of Arab-American studies at the University of Michigan, was one of those answering the question. In her communication, Professor Alsultany not only declared it her intention to pursue political agendas in the classroom but also made a veiled (and typically inverted) reference to the academic freedom campaign, which she complained was causing the pursuit of nonacademic agendas to be "more difficult":

> Date: 8/16/2006 3:47 PM
> From: Evelyn Alsultany <alsultan@umich.edu>
> Hi Jay,
>
> I personally think it is very important to address current politics and wars in our classes. Unfortunately, given the many attacks on academic freedom over the last few years, this has become more important and more difficult.
>
> I will not be teaching this Fall, but in the Winter semester I will be team teaching a course with Nadine Naber, "Why Do They Hate Us?: Perspectives on 9/11 . . ." The other course I will be teaching in the Winter is called, "From Harems to Terrorists: Representing the Middle East in Hollywood Cinema." While the focus is on U.S. media and particularly Hollywood films, the course more broadly examines the ideologies that justify anti-Arab racism and U.S.-led wars in the Middle East.

Another answer to the question was provided by Kyla Tompkins, assistant professor of English literature and women's studies at Pomona College, one of the premier liberal arts colleges in America.

> Date: 8/16/2006 2:16 PM
> From: Kyla Tompkins <kyla.tompkins@pomona.edu>

> In my feminist theory class, we spend the last two weeks on Feminism after 9/11 and students have responded really well to that. More pertinent to this list, I teach a Cultures of U.S. Imperialism class, mostly a 19th-century course, and the war is present in everything we talk about. One text that was particularly eerie was the Susannah Rowson text Slaves of Algiers, a text that uncannily echoed Bush's early "Save the Women in the Service of Democracy and Freedom" rhetoric during the beginning of the Afghanistan War. However we also paid a lot of attention to the proto (or is it para-?) Zionist rhetoric of many 19th-century texts and rhetoric.

(Note that Professor Tompkins has no academic credential or background that would qualify her to teach about imperialism, slavery, or Zionism. According to her faculty website, her "expertise areas" are: "Cultural Theory, American Studies, Food Studies, 19th Century U.S. Literature, Critical Feminism.")[6]

The use of classrooms for political agendas violates the specific regulations that most universities adopted following the 1940 statement on academic freedom. These regulations are published in faculty handbooks and posted on official university websites. Yet academic authorities were no longer enforcing them. Moreover, students affected by the infractions were generally unaware of the guidelines. Consequently, they had no way of knowing when teachers were behaving unprofessionally in the classroom and thus violating their academic freedom.

It occurred to me that once informed of the guidelines, students themselves could become an important factor in correcting the abuses. If it was the responsibility of faculty not to indoctrinate students, it should be the right of students not to be indoctrinated. If administrators were not enforcing their own guidelines, students might prod them to do so once they were informed of their rights. These were the ideas that gave rise to the academic freedom campaign. In drafting the Academic Bill of Rights, I articulated and codified the traditional principles as student rights. I then set about creating an organization, Students for Academic Freedom,[7] to promote these rights and to call for an end to the abuses.

The overarching goal of the academic freedom campaign was to end political advocacy by professors in their classrooms, regardless of whether their politics were left or right. It was also an effort to restore traditional academic standards that promoted scholarly neutrality and objectivity. The goals of the campaign expressed the long-held consensus about the purpose of a democratic education that had only recently come under attack—the purpose of publicly supported educational institutions in democracies was to create free citizens who were able to think for themselves and not to instill approved doctrines.

Since the Academic Bill of Rights was a liberal and viewpoint-neutral document, based on existing university standards, it should have won widespread, nonpartisan support among administrators and academics. It was my original plan, therefore, to seek broad-based support and to promote its adoption by universities. This should have been relatively easy, since the bill represented ideas to which they were already committed. Because my goal was to prevent the educational mission from being suborned by political interests, I was particularly concerned to respect the independence of the academic institutions and therefore to avoid legislative measures to implement the reforms.

On the other hand, it was obvious even before I began that political forces had already established themselves *inside* the university, and to such a degree that they could not be ignored. The presence of these political forces, whose aggressiveness had made it impossible for university administrators to implement the existing academic freedom guidelines, had created the problem to begin with.

University presidents were first and foremost fund-raisers, and open conflict with a significant segment of their faculties was not likely to advance their administrative careers. Nor could trustees step in to help them, since university boards were kept at arm's length by "shared governance" rules, which discouraged them from getting involved in curricular issues. In short, there appeared to be no authority inside the university able to enforce university rules in the face of determined faculty opposition. This meant that correcting the problem would require outside pressure.

If I did not fully understand these facts when I began my efforts, they were made apparent soon enough. I had drafted the Academic Bill of Rights specifically for adoption by the State University of New York, a system with 69 campuses and over 400,000 students. I did so after meeting with the chairman of its board of trustees, Tom Egan, in November 2002. Like other SUNY trustees, Egan had been appointed by Governor George Pataki, a Republican. He was well disposed towards my proposal and assured me that the Academic Bill of Rights would be adopted by the SUNY board. But it was a promise he proved unable to keep. As months passed and administrative paralysis set in, I realized that it was never going to happen. It was also evident that the factors preventing it from taking place were political to the core.

The most important of these factors was the political composition of the SUNY faculty, whose senate and professional associations were dominated by the activist left. As soon as the Academic Bill of Rights was published, the head of the SUNY teachers' union, representing thirty thousand professors and staff, denounced it as "crazy" and "Orwellian," and disparaged it with puerile humor as the "Academic Bull of Rights."[8] Although the bill specifically protected the political opinions of all professors, the union head pronounced it a McCarthy "witch-hunt." With political operatives like this leading the way, there was not the slightest chance that an Academic Bill of Rights would pass the SUNY Faculty Senate, or that Egan and the SUNY trustees would attempt to introduce such a policy over the union's opposition.

As many studies have recently revealed, the left-wing politics of the SUNY faculty were far from unique.[9] Thirty years of exclusionary hiring practices had led to a situation where university faculties across the country were stacked heavily to the left of the political spectrum. Self-described "liberals" outnumbered self-described "conservatives" by more than seven to one.[10] In fields like anthropology—and among junior faculty across the board—the figures already approached thirty to one.[11] It was probably the case that most professors, liberal or otherwise, were professional in their work and adhered to the principle of classroom neutrality. But a significant minority—representing tens of thousands of professors—regarded themselves as political activists first, and this overrode their professional concerns. Equally important, they were far more vocal and aggressive than their liberal peers, and as a result they dominated the organs of faculty power. This activist minority was ready to resist any attempt to enforce professional standards of conduct that might obstruct their political agendas, and to intimidate anyone who got in their way.

The organizational dominance of political activists was an academic development whose seeds had been planted in the 1960s and whose growth had accelerated in subsequent decades.[12] By the time the Academic Bill of Rights was proposed, these radicals had become so institutionally powerful that any effort to challenge their prerogatives risked precipitating a faculty revolt. The censure and subsequent resignation of Harvard president Larry Summers in the spring of 2006 was a classic example of how this faculty power could be mobilized to determine the outcome of political confrontations with administrators. The threat of such protests was enough to ensure that a university administration would take no action on a matter like the Academic Bill of Rights absent an external intervention.

The same fear affected trustees like SUNY's Tom Egan. The trustees of public universities were normally (though not always) appointed by governors whose political ambitions would be damaged if they collided with an academic senate or faculty union on such curricular issues. This was particularly true if the issue could be framed as "political." As their campaign against the Academic Bill of Rights showed, leftists were adept at doing just that when their own agendas—which, of course, were intensely political—were blocked. Thus an administrative attempt to *remove* politics from the curriculum would be opposed by faculty radicals as itself a political intervention *into* the curriculum. It was a Wonderland logic, but effective. The result was a paralysis of administrative will in matters concerning academic freedom. This was the explanation for the months that passed without action by the SUNY chairman on my proposal.

The impasse convinced me that I had no recourse but to take the issue to state legislatures, if only to rouse public opinion on the matter. Public concern could have an impact on university enrollments and the attitudes of funders, and represented forces that university administrators could not afford to ignore. My purpose was not to urge legislators to micromanage state universities, but to gain leverage that might help the university administrators enforce academic guidelines that were already in place. The legislation I eventually sought was exclusively in the form of resolutions, which lacked statutory "teeth" to enforce their provisions. My calculation was that even if legislatures only expressed a desire that existing standards be enforced, it would provide administrators with a persuasive argument for enforcing their own rules. The alternative was to let the ideal of academic freedom wither on the vine.

The practicality of this new plan—and the possibility of accomplishing its objectives without interfering with university governance—was soon demonstrated in the state of Colorado. In June 2003, I traveled to Denver to meet with Governor Bill Owens and a group of legislators to outline the problem. They were receptive to my ideas, and John Andrews, the majority leader of the Colorado Senate, agreed to sponsor the bill. Andrews subsequently turned the sponsorship over to Representative Shawn Mitchell after he realized he could not get it through the senate with a one-vote majority.

Like many legislatures, Colorado's sat only six months of the year, so it was not until March 2004 that a version of the Academic Bill of Rights was put before the Education Committee of the state house of representatives. It soon passed on a 6-5 party-line vote. Almost immediately, the heads of Colorado's state universities approached Mitchell with a request that he withdraw the bill if they would put the policy into effect. It was exactly the result I had desired. A "memorandum of understanding" was quickly signed by the parties concerned, and then a joint resolution endorsing the compromise was passed unanimously by both houses of Colorado's legislature.[13]

While this was a positive development, I already knew that the problem had never been *devising* an academic freedom policy, but *implementing* one. To enforce academic freedom guidelines would require goodwill by a broad spectrum of the parties involved, whether this meant university communities or legislatures. First there would have to be a nonpartisan recognition of the problem and then a consensus that it should be addressed. Unfortunately, the lobbying efforts of the professor unions and associations against the Academic Bill of Rights had already led to a situation that was so bitterly divided that no real consensus was possible. The Colorado Democrats voted for the joint resolution, but did so only to get rid of the issue. When Republicans lost control of the legislature the following November, the Democrats revealed their lack of interest in pressing the academic freedom agenda, and the opportunity to do something passed.[14]

The partisan attack that effectively killed the academic freedom reform effort was launched in Colorado even before the legislation was formally proposed.[15] Two months after my June visit, the *Rocky Mountain News* published a front-page story "exposing" the "secret" meetings I was alleged to have had with Governor Owens and the Republican legislators. In fact, far from being secret, my meeting with the governor took place in his office, while my breakfast with the legislators was held at the Brown Palace Hotel, perhaps the most famous venue and favorite meeting place for Denver's political elites. Both meetings were part of the normal civic process.

Despite my best efforts to present the academic freedom issue as nonpartisan, the inflammatory story in the *Rocky Mountain News* was headlined "GOP Takes On Leftist Education" and claimed that I was behind a right-wing plot to attack "liberals" on university faculties and create an affirmative action program that would force universities to hire conservatives.[16] Both accusations were false. I had anticipated such an attack and therefore designed the first principle of the Academic Bill of Rights to render such misrepresentations impossible (or so I thought): "No faculty shall be hired or fired or denied promotion or tenure on the basis of his or her political or religious beliefs." Thus the Academic Bill of Rights declared in as clear a manner as possible that no liberals could be fired for being liberals and no conservatives could be hired for being conservatives. But this didn't dissuade the *Rocky Mountain News* reporter, Peggy Lowe, who simply ignored the facts.[17]

I complained to the *News* editors and they agreed to print a correction of the article's false claims. Written by Vincent Carroll, editor of the paper's editorial page, it was titled "Tone the Rhetoric Down." Carroll pointed out that the Academic Bill of Rights proposed none of the measures that Lowe's story "reported." Instead, "the Academic Bill of Rights advocates precisely the opposite of political litmus tests." In the same edition, the *News* also printed excerpts from the bill to prove the point.

This was the good news. The bad news was that Colorado's other major paper, the *Denver Post,* decided to ignore the *News's* correction and run a lead editorial repeating the false charge: "The same party that's been squawking over race-based college admissions now apparently wants universities to check voter-registration rolls when hiring faculty to ensure more conservatives are added to the ranks."[18] There were no facts to substantiate this claim, but it was the *Post* editorial rather than the *Rocky Mountain News* correction that set the precedent for columns and editorials throughout the state.[19] Typical was a *Post* column that appeared a day later, written by former Democratic lieutenant governor Gail Schoettler, titled "Mind Police Are At It Again."[20]

Such false claims became the core of the opposition to the academic freedom campaign, and were repeated over and over in the face of all efforts to correct them. In addition to grossly misrepresenting the campaign's agenda, opponents directed their attacks at its supporters, in particular myself. Although I had designed the Academic Bill of Rights to *end* an existing black-list,[21] promote a diversity of intellectual views, and take politics out of the classroom, I was routinely smeared as a reincarnation of Senator Joseph McCarthy, a "witch-hunter," and a *promoter* of political intrusions into academic life. On one fanciful leftist web-site, I was portrayed as Mao Zedong, whose Cultural Revolution in China featured the persecution of professors by Maoist students for straying from the party line.[22] An irony in the attack was that Mao originated the term "political correctness," and those who made the analogy and were old enough to have played a role in the Sixties had supported Mao's Cultural Revolution when it took place. Nonetheless, tens of thousands of references linking me to witch-hunters soon appeared on the Internet.[23]

While dishonest tactics like this have come to rule the academic freedom debate, I understand that there can be reasonable disagreement on the issues and that there are honest critics of what I have proposed. One such is Stanley Fish, a distinguished Milton scholar, law professor and First Amendment expert, and a well-known academic liberal. Professor Fish's writings on academic freedom had already influenced the academic freedom campaign, particularly his argument that universities should maintain institutional neutrality with respect to controversies that divide the larger community.[24] I incorporated this principle into the Academic Bill of Rights and also benefited from his explanation of the distinction between academic freedom, which is freedom within a professional discipline, and "free speech," which entails no such professional obligations.[25] Finally, he has articulated the critical distinction between academic discourse and political pros-elytizing with particular clarity: "Any idea can be brought into the classroom if the point is to inquire into its structure, history, influence and so forth. But no idea belongs in the classroom if the point of introducing it is to recruit your students for the polit-ical agenda it may be thought to imply."[26]

Despite our agreement on these key issues, Professor Fish has opposed the legislative agendas of the campaign and, on occa-sion, has opposed versions of the Academic Bill of Rights itself. In May 2006, for example, he criticized a version of the bill that had recently been passed in the student referendum at Prince-ton. In Professor Fish's view, the goals specified in the Princeton document—academic freedom and intellectual diversity—were mutually exclusive. "The strong suggestion is that academic free-dom and intellectual diversity go together, but in fact they pull in opposite directions," he argued. "Academic freedom is the freedom to go wherever an intellectual inquiry takes you with-out regard to directives proclaimed in advance by a regime of prior restraint. Intellectual diversity is a prior restraint; it tells you where to look and what you must look at—you must take into account every point of view independently of whether you think it is worth considering—and it tells you what materials you must include in your syllabus."[27]

Professor Fish's objection is mistaken on several counts. First, there is no implication in either the Princeton bill or the Aca-demic Bill of Rights that intellectual diversity requires that a cur-riculum include every point of view, let alone points of view that are not worth considering.[28] The principle of intellectual diver-sity merely proposes that in controversial matters more than one legitimate conclusion is always possible. Teachers should make their students aware of this by including dissenting views (or even *a* dissenting view) in their reading lists and in their discourse. The points of view included should reflect "significant scholarly opin-ion" (as the Academic Bill of Rights specifies) and not just any opinion however extreme.

The idea behind the principle is that there should be no preexisting classroom orthodoxies and therefore no "politically correct" conclusions about controversial issues. This is the fundamental assumption of a democracy. If there were one correct conclusion to such controversies, there would be no need for a multiparty system. The only party required would be the one in possession of the Truth. No such Truth Party exists. There are no Truth Departments and no Truth Professors. Consequently, the principle of intellectual diversity and respect for political difference is basic to those academic subjects—the humanities and the social sciences—that inevitably address controversial issues. There is no orthodoxy on controversial matters that would be appropriate for professors to enforce in the classroom or to impose on the students they teach. That is a principle which until relatively recently was regarded as self-evident. The Academic Bill of Rights is designed to make the principle clear and thus to ensure the absence of such orthodoxies in the classroom.

I doubt that Professor Fish would disagree with these views. His criticism of the Academic Bill of Rights can be traced, rather, to suspicions about the motives of its supporters, particularly legislators, and his concerns about the way the Princeton document was worded. Such suspicions could probably be allayed and his concerns accommodated in a less polarized political atmosphere than presently exists.

Professor Fish's second point, on the other hand, evokes a difference that is central to the argument itself. He maintains that academic freedom is "the freedom to go wherever an intellectual inquiry takes you without regard to directives proclaimed in advance by a regime of prior restraint." If this is meant to refer to academic research, it is quite correct. But if it is meant to apply to classroom discourse, Professor Fish has already described the restrictions that apply: classroom discourse must be professional and academic.

During a visit I made to Penn State University just prior to the Princeton referendum, the inability to comprehend this point was made clear in the remarks of students who opposed my appearance. I was invited to speak on the subject of academic freedom, and the Penn State College Democrats protested my speech. What educational value was served by protesting a speech on academic freedom before it was delivered? Why not listen to the speaker and then respond? Why not organize a debate? The Democrats' protest was just one more indication of how the public forums at universities like Penn State had become more akin to political battlegrounds than to neutral and intellectually inviting settings where ideas are examined and evaluated in an academic manner.

In explaining why his group was protesting my talk, the chairman of the College Democrats claimed that my campaign was an attempt to *restrict* professors' speech and, in his view, academic freedom meant that professors had the right "to say anything they want in the classroom."[29] On both points this young man was dead wrong. My campaign proposed no new restrictions on professors' speech, and Penn State's own academic freedom policies already specifically restricted what Penn State professors might say in the classroom.

Penn State's academic freedom policy is set forth in its *Policy Manual*. Policy HR 64 says this:

> No faculty member may claim as a right the privilege of discussing in the classroom controversial topics outside his/her own field of study. The faculty member is normally bound not to take advantage of his/her position by introducing into the classroom provocative discussions of irrelevant subjects not within the field of his/her study.

This is a pretty clear restriction, designed to ensure that the classroom discourse of faculty members is professional, remains in their area of expertise and does not include extraneous matters that are introduced for political reasons. However, at the time of my visit, as discussions with the students who invited me revealed, this principle was being violated regularly by Penn State professors who thought nothing of attacking President Bush, the war in Iraq and Republicans generally in classes that had nothing to do with the president, the war in Iraq or the Republican Party.

Penn State's academic freedom policy further elaborates:

> The faculty member is entitled to freedom in the classroom in discussing his/her subject. The faculty member is, however, responsible for the maintenance of appropriate standards of scholarship and teaching ability. It is not the function of a faculty member in a democracy to indoctrinate his/her students with ready-made conclusions on controversial subjects. The faculty member is expected to train students to think for themselves, and to provide them access to those materials, which they need if they are to think intelligently. Hence, in giving instruction upon controversial matters the faculty member is expected to be of a fair and judicial mind, and to set forth justly, without super-cession or innuendo, the divergent opinions of other investigators.[30]

These restrictions—that professors should not engage in controversial advocacy outside their fields of expertise and must not "indoctrinate ... students with ready-made conclusions on controversial subjects"—are the cornerstones of a professional education in a democracy and make up the core doctrine of academic freedom as it has been understood and accepted by the academic profession for nearly a hundred years. It is a sad commentary on the present state of affairs that the students who tried to preempt my speech were not aware of their own university's foundational documents.

Nor is this view of academic freedom idiosyncratic, or a merely conservative position. Robert Post, a liberal law professor at Yale, is one of the nation's leading experts on academic freedom issues and legal counsel to the American Association of University Professors. In a seminal article on "The Structure of Academic Freedom," Professor Post observed: "[A] key premise of the '1915 Declaration' is that faculty should be regarded as professional experts in the production of knowledge."[31] Professor Post explains this premise: "The mission of the university defended by the 'Declaration,' depends on a particular theory of knowledge. The 'Declaration' presupposes not only that knowledge exists and can be articulated by scholars, but also that it is advanced through the free application of highly disciplined forms of inquiry, which correspond roughly to what [philosopher] Charles Pierce once called 'the method of science' as opposed to the 'method of authority.'" Post continues: "The 'Declaration' claims that universities can advance the sum of human knowledge only if they employ persons who are experts in scholarly methods, and only if universities liberate these experts to pursue freely the inquiries dictated by their disciplinary training."[32] In other words: submission to a regime of prior (professional) restraint is the very basis of the academic freedom privileges to which professors are entitled.

It is because their mission depends on the hiring of professionals that universities require an academic credential—the Ph.D.—which is a certification that the faculty hired are trained and disciplined professionals in their fields.[33] The implication (in the words of the 1915 Declaration) is this: "[The] liberty of the scholar within the university to set forth his conclusions, be they what they may, is conditioned by their being conclusions gained by a scholar's method and held in a scholar's spirit; that is to say, they must be the fruits of competent and patient and sincere inquiry...." Or, as Post summarizes it: "The 'Declaration' thus conceives of academic freedom not as an individual right to be free from constraints but instead as the freedom to pursue the 'scholar's profession' according to the standards of that profession."[34]

In other words, academic freedom does imply restraint— the restraint of disciplined and professional standards of inquiry and expression. The attempt to ignore or bypass this restraint threatens the integrity of the academic mission. In doing so, it also threatens the university as an institution. When universities allow their faculties to enter the political fray by becoming opinionated partisans in the academic classroom, they expose themselves and their institutions to the laws of the political arena, and to its judgments and penalties as well.

Members of the public who find themselves on the other side of political disputes from university faculties will take a different attitude towards their classroom behavior than they would towards controversial positions they adopt that are professional and express an academic expertise. They will rightly defer to the academic experts on such academic matters. But when academics appear as political partisans in the university setting, members of the lay public will consider themselves equals. If they find that the institution they are supporting is a political actor on the other side of a controversial issue, their enthusiasm for supporting that institution will correspondingly diminish. It may be regarded as a law of politics that one doesn't finance one's opponents.

These considerations have already become a significant problem and not just for the University of Colorado, which lost tens of millions of dollars as a result of the adverse publicity generated by ethnic studies professor Ward Churchill's attacks on the victims of 9/11 in the winter of 2005. At an academic freedom conference I organized in April 2006, Senator Lamar Alexander, a former secretary of education, was a featured speaker. Senator Alexander, a moderate Republican and lifelong supporter of federal aid to education, said: "The greatest threat to the American university today—to broad public support for the American university today—is political one-sidedness from the left, and that's a serious threat because if you look at the funding trends for higher education, federal funding is up, but state funding is flat, and tuition is up as a result of that. And constantly inferior funding by the states of higher education will produce substandard universities, and that will produce substandard incomes for the rest of us. So for the strength of the university, for the expression of free thought, your movement needs to succeed."[35]

An example of the adverse public reactions that can be caused by political intrusions into the university curriculum occurred in the state of Pennsylvania in the early summer of 2003. State representative Gib Armstrong, who served as a Marine in Mogadishu before entering politics, was approached at a Republican Party picnic by a constituent who wanted to talk to him about a physics class she was taking at one of Pennsylvania's public universities. The constituent was an Air Force veteran of the war in Iraq. On returning from active duty, she had enrolled at a Penn State campus to finish her education. But in class she found herself subject to harangues by her professor on the evils of the military and the war in which she had just served. She asked Representative Armstrong if such an attack was appropriate to a physics classroom.

Armstrong then contacted me and the result was legislation HR 177 in the Pennsylvania House of Representatives, creating a "Select Committee on Academic Freedom in Higher Education in Pennsylvania." During the academic year 2005–2006, the committee held a series of hearings on the state of academic freedom in Pennsylvania's public colleges and universities, which led directly to the first university adoption of an academic bill of rights.[36]

TWO

A Revealing Debate

In the 1950s, universities were referred to as "ivory towers," a phrase often used in a derogatory manner but in hindsight reflecting a shrewd determination to insulate themselves from the political currents roiling the nonacademic world. In all my years at Columbia and my graduate years later at Berkeley, I never heard a professor express a political point of view in a classroom or in any campus setting. Even in the early 1960s, when student radicals like myself had begun to organize campus political movements, my professors continued to maintain their scholarly distance. It was not until a decade later, when Sixties activists had themselves become faculty, that radical politics began to make their appearance in the academic curriculum. At the same time, professorial activism began to become an integral feature of university life.

By the time I began speaking on campuses at the end of the 1980s, these changes were already evident. By then, the academic community had become a zone of agitation in a way that would have been unthinkable to earlier generations. Universities were now the setting for a prodigious array of political activities and were often institutionally supportive of their agendas. Causes like "social justice" were even inscribed in the mission statements of entire departments. More often than not, the campus leaders of these political causes were members of the faculty. In parallel with these developments, there was a visibly diminishing presence of conservatives on faculties, as older generations retired and conservative replacements were not hired.

These new attitudes translated into an institutional hostility to conservative speakers visiting campus. As one of them, I rarely arrived at a school without being identified in advance as a "controversial" figure, which meant that I constituted a threat to the prejudices that faculty had designated "politically correct." When I addressed three hundred students at the University of Chicago in 2006, for example, the school's student activities coordinator, who was present, never introduced herself to me. Instead, she stepped to the microphone before I spoke to inform students that a "safe room" was available for anyone who might need it— in other words, relief was at hand for anyone traumatized by what I might have to say. Needless to say, no such safe room was provided during speeches by the many left-wing radicals who came to the same campus.[1]

I was hardly alone in being labeled toxic by college administrators or targeted by protesters as someone against whom college students needed to be immunized. Raucous demonstrations both outside and inside the auditoriums where conservatives spoke were almost routine. In 2005, I was one of several conservative speakers physically attacked while attempting to deliver a campus address. At Butler University, a group of demonstrators barged into a speech I was giving and shoved a cream pie in my face. While I suffered no harm, the experience could hardly be counted benign. The suit I was wearing was drenched and my hair was syrupy and matted as I was forced to deliver my remarks in a somewhat sorry-looking state. Moreover, the pie, shoved in the area of my eye, might have done actual damage if it had a little more force behind it. Because of such attacks and the anger they exposed, I found it prudent to hire a bodyguard, whom I shared with Ann Coulter and Michelle Malkin, two other targets of campus hate.

While invitations to conservatives almost invariably came from conservative student groups, faculty and administrators generally avoided the events and often actively boycotted them. In a typical case at Cal State Monterey Bay, I was approached by a student who had written a paper critical of the Academic Bill of Rights, and who told me that his teacher had warned him not to hear what I had to say because I was "too right-wing." Similarly, when conservative students invited me to speak at the University of California, Berkeley, Chancellor Robert Berdahl told a *Los Angeles Times* reporter that I had "provoked a dialogue that no one wanted to hear," and refused to provide an administrator to introduce the event.[2] Instead he assigned thirty armed guards to maintain order. At more than one university, professors circulated flyers and e-mails insinuating that I was a "racist" because of my opposition to left-wing proposals like race preferences or slave reparations 135 years after the fact.[3]

Student governments, dominated by the left, regularly refused to fund conservative speakers, but they provided generous honorariums to radicals.[4] When radicals came to campus, faculty often required students to attend their presentations, offering them academic credits to do so. Left-wing speakers were also frequently invited by academic departments and administrations who used administrative funds to underwrite their appearances— which was one reason why their events were far more frequent than those featuring conservatives. It was not unusual, in fact, for a conservative speaker to be the only conservative invited to a given campus over a period of years. In a not untypical case, at Emory University in Georgia I was the first conservative speaker in four years. At Cal State Monterey Bay, which had been designated a "social justice campus" by university administrators, I was the first conservative speaker invited in the eleven-year history of the school.[5]

It was also not unusual for the university welcome mat to be laid out for speakers who were far more radical on the left side of the spectrum than I was as a conservative. This included extremists like Ward Churchill, who notoriously claimed that the 9/11 terrorist attacks were justified, and whom professors lined

up to honor; or Communists like Angela Davis and former terrorist leader Bernadine Dohrn, who are also icons in the academic community. Like Churchill, Davis and Dohrn are often
featured speakers at official university programs—Dohrn, for
example, at the commencement at Pitzer College in 2005 and
Davis at Martin Luther King Days at various prestigious schools.
Nor is it unusual to have their student-sponsored speeches attended
by university officials who come to welcome them to campus
and honor them as distinguished guests.

Given these circumstances, it was an unexpected pleasure
to be invited to Reed University in the fall of 2005 by a faculty
committee, and to be accorded the honor of debating the dean
of faculty on a formal university occasion like Parents and Fam-
ily Day. The pleasure was enhanced by my awareness of Reed's
reputation for left-wing politics, which dated back to before the
Sixties era.

The topic for debate was the Academic Bill of Rights. I
arrived on campus early for a tour that included a meeting with
Reed's president, Colin Diver, one of several university presidents who had agreed to meet with me that year. I attributed
this new receptivity to the success of the academic freedom campaign in promoting the intellectual diversity issue. Fairness and
intellectual pluralism were values that transcended political divi-
sions. The publicity surrounding these campaigns had put administrators who shunned conservatives like me in an increasingly
untenable position.

The meeting with President Diver and the reception he
gave me were welcome departures from the many years I had
spent out in the university cold. Our conversation revealed that
Diver was sympathetic to my concerns about academic freedom,
while professionally cautious about committing himself to specific reforms. I also met with a political science professor, Paul
Gronke, the faculty member who had extended the invitation.
Gronke was the kind of liberal I recalled from my college days—
tolerant, scholarly and professional. It was a notable contrast to

the professors I had become used to, who generally put up a wall of hostility to those they disagreed with, while continuing to refer to themselves as "liberal."

When I asked Gronke to explain his invitation, he told me that he had extended it out of respect for my intellectual work and because the issues I raised were important and worthy of discussion. I was so unaccustomed to respect from faculty that I pressed him further to see if he wasn't actually a closet conservative. He laughed and said, "No. I would vote for Donald Duck if he were the Democrat."

A lunch was arranged where I was able to meet with a dozen Reed students, an occasion I found equally encouraging. The students were bright and earnest, and our discussion focused exclusively on intellectual issues, which was also a surprise. When the session finally came to an end, I still had no idea of the politics of the individual students, which was exactly how an academic conversation should take place.

This experience caused me to inquire about the curriculum at Reed, which had produced such thoughtful responses. I learned that Reed's course offerings were quite traditional. For example, literary texts were taught as literature, as they should be—not as coded politics or as pretexts for explicating radical ideology, as they often were at the other schools I had visited. It did not surprise me to learn that there were no trendy politicized departments such as Women's Studies or Black Studies or Peace Studies at Reed. The more I inquired, the more Reed's academic program was pleasantly reminiscent of the education I had received at Columbia College half a century before.

My debate with the dean of faculty, Peter Steinberger, was scheduled for the afternoon. Steinberger had been on the Reed faculty for nearly thirty years and had served as Reed's acting president for two. His resumé seemed to place him on the left, but the titles of his publications revealed no particularly political agenda. In an interview about intellectual diversity that had appeared in one of the school's publications, he remarked that he did not allow his political views to intrude into his lessons. All these indicators augured well for the proceedings to follow.

Under the prearranged debate format, I was allotted the first twenty minutes to state my case. I began by praising the college and its students. Noting its reputation as a "leftist school," I said my conversations that day had revealed a Reed refreshingly different from the one I had been led to expect. Far from offering a menu of ideological courses, I said, "the curriculum here is quite excellent. It's quite traditional, classical. It's academic as it should be, and I want to compliment the school on that. Moreover, I have met with a dozen Reed students today and found them to be an extraordinarily bright and surprisingly independent-minded group of young people who are able to think for themselves and who *think* rather than reacting emotionally to intellectual challenges, as unfortunately many universities have primed their students to do."[6]

From there, I proceeded to the substance of my case. The Academic Bill of Rights was designed to promote two agendas— "intellectual diversity" and "academic manners." By the latter I meant that differing viewpoints should be accorded proper intellectual respect. Too often, when conservative ideas were introduced, it was to a chorus of derision which professors either instigated or condoned. This was an indefensible intimidation of conservative students, while it relieved liberal students and professors alike of the burden of constructing an intellectual response. Yet this was precisely what "higher learning" ought to be about.

I introduced the subject of intellectual diversity by sharing my positive impressions of Reed students with the parents in attendance. But I also indicated my concern about the missing conservative component in Reed's academic mix. As at other schools, there were virtually no conservative professors on the Reed faculty, which made the achievement of academic excellence an almost impossible task. "You can't get a good education"—I repeated one of my tag lines—"if they're only telling you half the story, even if you're paying $40,000 a year," which was the tuition fee at Reed.

I used my lunch meeting with Reed students to underscore the point. Only two of the twelve students present at the meeting had ever heard of a major conservative intellectual like Thomas Sowell, who, as I told them, was "the foremost thinker on issues of culture and race in this country, and certainly one of the most formidable intellects alive in America." I told them it was "disgraceful" that only two students had ever heard of Professor Sowell, particularly since all twelve of the students I had met were majoring in the humanities and social sciences.

I had also asked the students how many of them had read anything by Friedrich Hayek, a libertarian thinker on political and economic issues who had won the Nobel Prize. Only two had ever read or been assigned a text by Hayek. But every hand went up when I asked how many students had been required to read a book by Noam Chomsky—a linguistics professor at MIT, whose voluminous writings on current events had nothing to do with his academic expertise. In fact, Chomsky is a radical whose animus against his own country is so great that he has described the attack on Pearl Harbor as "a good thing" and warned in his most recent book that the "American empire" is a threat to "global survival."[7] In other words, an opinionated text without scholarly value by Noam Chomsky was considered more worthy of assignment by Reed's "liberal" professors than a text by Hayek, one of the foremost academic intellects of the century, who happened to be a "conservative."[8]

When I had spoken for twenty minutes, the moderator signaled that my time was up. I brought my presentation to a close with a plea to Reed students "to get the Academic Bill of Rights adopted as a policy at this school, and to press your faculty and your administration to bring professors to this campus who are conservatives.... If you do that ... you will have much more interesting conversations and you will learn even more than you are learning now."

The audience gave my presentation a respectful reception. Stepping down from the podium, I took a seat in the front to listen to what my opponent had to say. Dean Steinberger mounted the stage and placed a sheaf of papers on the lectern. "I didn't think I was going to be the villain in this event when it began," he said ominously, "but I think I'm going to be."[9] It was an odd way to begin, and he followed it with this: "I have come to the conclusion that you simply cannot understand the Academic Bill of Rights unless you understand the body of work out of which it emerges. So, I'm going to say some things about that. I'm going to say some tough things about that." And tough things he did say, mainly about me.

To have the terms of debate suddenly altered—so that the issue is no longer the issue, but something that "explains" the issue—is a typical experience for anyone engaging opponents on the left. To have the subject shifted to oneself is equally inevitable. Often it is one's alleged "privilege," derived from racial origins or class position, that becomes the new focus of attack. But whatever the approach, the issue ultimately settles on one's alleged deficiency. Being a conservative is itself such a deficiency. This is the prosecutorial stance that makes up the core of the progressives' worldview. It is a reminder to themselves and to anyone listening that they are engaged in a battle of good versus evil, and that there cannot be two decent sides to the debates they are engaged in. Consequently, although the tirade that followed was an ad hominem attack on me, I tried not to take it too personally.

For the next forty minutes, while the frustrated moderator strove vainly to enforce the time limit, Dean Steinberger proceeded with the indictment he had prepared. For page after page, he read from a text that until the last ten minutes did not even address the Academic Bill of Rights. Instead, for paragraph after paragraph his text savaged my character and impugned my integrity in an attempt to discredit anything I had to say. It was simply a bid to eliminate my position from the discussion entirely. The cause of vanquishing an ideological adversary was apparently so important to Dean Steinberger that it overwhelmed every other consideration including that of civility, and even self-interest.

His remarks continued with a disingenuous disclaimer, deny-
ing exactly what he was about to do: "My goal is not personally
to attack Mr. Horowitz. I just met him a few minutes ago. He's
a genial fellow, said nice things about Reed, I appreciate that.
My goal is not to be unfriendly to a guest to this campus." Having dispensed with the throat clearing, he proceeded directly to
the demolition:

"Let me begin by looking at a book that Mr. Horowitz published in the year 2000, titled *The Art of Political War.*" (This was
actually a small pamphlet I had written in 1998 and then included
as the opening chapter of a book by the same title a year or so
later. It was a short manual for political campaigns, and not at all
about educational reform. But it had been praised by presidential adviser Karl Rove, which was perhaps all the incitement that
Steinberger needed. This was the "body of work," he claimed,
that provided the key to understanding my thoughts about academic freedom and the Academic Bill of Rights.)[10]

"Horowitz says that politics is war by other means," said
Steinberger. "And just as all's fair in love and war, so too in political war. In political war, you say whatever it takes to win or at
least anything that you can get away with. So political war is a
matter of, I'm quoting here, 'Spin,' 'deceit,' 'hypocrisy' and 'doubletalk.' 'Unprincipled lies.' 'Smear campaigns' and other 'dirty
tricks.' In political war, argument, evidence and truth are irrelevant. Horowitz is pretty explicit about this. The facts don't matter. The only thing that matters is winning. There are no scruples
and truth is unimportant. I emphasize, this is not according to
me, this is explicitly according to Horowitz. . . ."

In fact, Steinberger was not quoting anything I had actually
written. All this was explicitly according to *Steinberger,* and *not*
according to me. My "advice" as he summarized it, including the
"explicit" quotes he provided, was an invention. I have never said,
either in this book or anywhere else, that it is my point of view that
"all's fair" in political war; nor have I ever acted on the principle
of "whatever it takes to win," or advised anyone else to do so. The

words and phrases "spin," "deceit," "unprincipled lies" and "dirty tricks" do not appear anywhere in my text. The words "hypocrisy" and "doubletalk" do appear once, but in a passage referring to *Democrats,* not conservatives: "Of course, the Democrat campaign in defense of the President [during the Clinton impeachment] was a remarkable display of hypocrisy and double-talk...." The term "smear" or "smear campaign" does appear in my book—four times—but every one of these references is to a *Democratic* smear campaign against Republicans—never in a sentence advising Republicans to adopt a smear strategy towards Democrats, and never as a tactic advocated by me as a weapon of political war.

Having invented this incriminating dossier, Steinberger proceeded to judgment: "So, I hypothesize, engaging in political warfare, doing and saying whatever it takes to win, this is what Mr. Horowitz does for a living. It's his job, it's his way of life. And, of course, if this is true, then clearly what it means is that *it's simply impossible to take anything he says or does seriously, including anything he says today.* On his own account, on his own account of political warfare, I emphasize not my account, his own account, analysis means nothing, facts mean nothing, evidence means nothing and, of course, if we know this, if we know that Mr. Horowitz himself is a political warrior, then we'd be idiots if we listened seriously to anything he says." (Emphasis added.)

In other words, according to the dean of faculty and some-time acting president of the college—and before an audience unfamiliar with me or my work, and without arguing the actual intellectual issues of the debate—I was a devious and dishonest rogue, so Machiavellian by habit and by nature that only idiots would even listen to what I had to say, while my appearance on Reed's platform could presumably have come about only as the result of some catastrophic mistake.

"Political warfare"—in the sense defined in my pamphlet—is not, in fact, what I do for a living, and is certainly not my "way of life." The "politics" to which *The Art of Political War* is addressed is *electoral* politics (or politics before masses), which would not include the controversies I normally engage in as a public intellectual or in the many other books I have written, or in the academic freedom campaign itself. In fact, I have never myself been officially part of an electoral campaign, and my advice in this area is confined to a series of pamphlets, independently published during the election years 1998, 2000 and 2002.[11]

I have written many lengthy articles about academic freedom which have appeared in venues like the *Chronicle of Higher Education* and *InsideHigherEd.com*. Dean Steinberger discussed none of them. Instead, he focused his lengthy prefatory remarks on a manual designed for electoral campaigns and characterized me as someone who was "a political warrior ... [who] says simply whatever he thinks will work."

Throughout this line of commentary, which lasted more than twenty minutes, Steinberger made it seem as though the idea that politics is war conducted by other means originated with me. In fact, my book argued just the opposite. As stated quite clearly, the idea originated with the political left and in my view was its preferred strategy. Republicans, I argued, are disadvantaged when they do not recognize that a political war *already exists* and is being waged by the Democrats: "Here are the principles of political war *that the left understands* but conservatives do not...."[12] (Emphasis added.)

Moreover, I explained the strategy that I was proposing in the following (non-Machiavellian) way: "Republicans do not understand (as Democrats do) that politics is war conducted by other means; that it is a war of position; and that you can only win by linking your agendas directly to the interests of women, children, minorities, working Americans and the poor."[13] Of course, telling Republicans to care more about women, children, minorities and poor people—which is the actual message of my little book— would not make such a convenient target for Steinberger to attack.

The kind of tactical advice I give in *The Art of Political War* relates almost exclusively to electoral contests, which rely heavily on thirty-second TV commercials:

> You have only 30 seconds to make your point. Even if you had time
> to develop an argument, the audience you need to reach (the unde-
> cided and those in the middle who are not paying much attention)
> wouldn't get it.... Worse, while you've been making your argument
> the other side has already painted you as a mean-spirited, border-
> line racist controlled by religious zealots, securely in the pockets of
> the rich. Nobody who sees you this way is going to listen to you in
> any case. You're politically dead.[14]

My point here (and elsewhere in this pamphlet) is simple: If you
don't recognize the nature of the battlefield you are on, then your
opponents *who already view politics as war* are going to bury you,
even as you are trying to make your intellectual case. This is a
pretty good description of what happened to me at Reed at the
hands of Dean Steinberger. Apparently he regarded our academic
discussion as political war, which I did not. In other words, in
our debate I fit a type of Republican I had described—I was an
innocent abroad and didn't see the attack coming.

It was an irony, unnoticed by Steinberger, that the summary
lesson I had learned in leaving the ranks of the political left twenty-
five years before was almost the opposite of what he imputed to
me. The lesson I learned was to *reject* the Leninist vision of politics as apocalyptic warfare. This vision flowed inexorably from
the radical belief in a redeemed social future. If the object of
political activity is a new millennium, what means would not be
justified to achieve that end? Conservatives are not believers in
utopian redemption, but radicals are—which is why they are
seduced into thinking the end justifies the means. The rejection
of this radical belief in a world transformed was the very foundation of my conservative perspective. I wrote as much and in
so many words in the following passage, which appeared in *The
Art of Political War* but which apparently escaped Dean Steinberger's attention:

> Many people confuse politics and religion. Politics is the art of the
> possible. Religion is the pursuit of an ideal. In religious matters,
> integrity of principle is not only an advantage it is the goal itself.

Religion is not about getting tax cuts or building schools. It is about saving souls. Being virtuous and right, having integrity and standing on principle are the very essence of its agendas. You can't compromise with the devil and expect to get to heaven. In politics, on the other hand, pacts with the devil are made all the time, and on both sides of the political aisle. This can even be regarded as a healthy development. The 20th century is littered with the corpses of people who got in the way of politicians—Hitler, Lenin, Pol Pot—who thought they were on a religious mission of social redemption. The appropriate places for making people moral and good are churches and synagogues and mosques, not state houses or congressional hearing rooms.[15]

I don't think I could have made this any clearer. Do these observations sound like the views of a heartless Machiavelli? Does this look like advice to engage in all-out, no-holds-barred, ends-justify-the means aggression? On the contrary: everything I believe about politics flows from the perception that progressive missionaries like Lenin—and radicals like him who believe in absolute agendas to save the world—are dangerous and destructive. As a conservative, I am in fact—and despite some hard edges—a process liberal, and everything I have supported in my campaign for academic freedom is a testament to that.

It is not my purpose in pointing this out to conduct an exercise in self-justification, or to continue the Reed College debate *post hoc.* My purpose is to show how the opposition to the campaign for academic freedom is a classic project of the political left—and this is a key to understanding the passions that attend it. There could hardly be a more striking expression of the damage this left has done to the liberal idea of the university than the fact that the scorched-earth partisan in a debate about academic freedom at a prestigious liberal arts school was the liberal dean of its faculty.

The fact that Steinberger is not a political activist or a radical illustrates an important point about progressive politics generally. The rudeness towards others, the disrespect for opponents, the disposition to ad hominem attacks that are all hallmarks of progressive discourse are not quirks of individual character among people attracted to its agendas. They flow, rather, from the fundamental belief of leftists in a transformed future, a humanity that can be redeemed. If one's opponents stand in the way of this future— a future that will establish equality, compassion, peace, social justice—then why respect them? They are reactionary and malevolent. It is one's progressive responsibility, therefore, not to let one's instincts for civility obstruct the righteousness of one's cause.

Despite this, a regard for manners and respect for difference were not absent from Reed that day. Dean Steinberger's attack backfired severely. After the debate, students, parents and faculty all voiced their dismay at his behavior. Reaction to his rudeness was so great that the dean offered to resign his post, and within days of my departure I received formal apologies from President Diver and—somewhat grudgingly—from Dean Steinberger himself.

> November 8, 2005
> Dear David:
>
> I write, on behalf of Reed College, and on my own behalf, to extend my apologies to you for the way in which you were treated at Saturday's forum on the Academic Bill of Rights. In particular, I am referring, of course, to remarks made by Peter Steinberger in response to your opening statement. . . . We at Reed pride ourselves in engaging in vigorous debate and encouraging spirited disagreement on the merits of important issues. But we also pride ourselves on maintaining basic civility of discourse and hospitality to invited guests. In my view, the unexpected focus of Peter's remarks, and their harsh and personal tone, violated that expectation.
>
> As president of this school, a school I love, it pains me to see the school represented in this fashion. In my job, I am constantly challenged to see the "teachable moment" in unexpected or difficult situations. This incident has already proved to be an invaluable teachable moment at Reed, and will continue to be so for some time to come. Thank you again for coming to Reed, and participating so graciously in a very important—albeit, unfortunately difficult— discussion of a very important issue.
> Sincerely,
> Colin S. Diver

A day earlier, I had received this apology from Dean Steinberger:

From: Peter Steinberger
To: [David Horowitz]
Cc: [Colin Diver]
Sent: Monday, November 07, 2005 1:23 PM
Monday, November 7

I've thought a lot about Saturday's event. My thoughts are complex. Lots of people at Reed are angry at me, and I understand that. They feel that I represented the institution poorly. I'd like to share with you, as honestly and openly as I can, some of my thoughts:

If I was uncivil, personally abusive, or *ad hominem,* I apologize. This is a sincere apology. If I was personally abusive, that was not my intention and that's not my way of doing things. In fact, I do not believe that I said anything of that nature. I recall no *ad hominem* statements. But if I made them, I'm truly story....

You and others in attendance are, however, also free to question my judgment. The President of the college has done so in the most severe terms.... I intend to find some way of sharing this message with the entire Reed community. I have also told the President of my willingness, in the wake of this situation, to resign from my position as Dean, if this is what he desires.

Steinberger did not resign (nor would I have wished him to), and five months later *Reed Magazine* ran a retrospective article headlined, "Steinberger v. Horowitz: The Great Debacle?" The account, written by a student politically sympathetic to Steinberger, described me as "Horowitz the provocateur," even though—by Steinberger's own account—I had done nothing to provoke the attack. The writer questioned whether my rebuttal following Steinberger's long attack had gone "over the top" (in defending myself I took more than the allotted five minutes and gave an account of my views of liberalism and progressive politics generally). But the *Reed* article also asked whether "the Dean [was] fair in labeling Horowitz a 'political pornographer,' prone to citing technical truths in order to tell substantive lies."

In the article's conclusion, Steinberger made a statement that was as revealing as the ambivalent apology letter in demonstrating that his understanding of the episode remained irretrievably obtuse: "I was candid. I called it the way I saw it. I tried to focus not on Horowitz's person or character but on his published words. I tried to do my homework. I tried to support every claim with evidence—and in doing so I believed, and continue to believe, that I was showing respect for the audience, for the event, for the organizers and, yes, for Mr. Horowitz himself."

It was not clear to me how one showed "respect" for an opponent by calling him a "political pornographer," or how Steinberger could claim this was not a personal attack. The censure that the Reed community placed on his behavior, on the other hand, was a welcome reflection of its concern for the academic environment and dismay over the disrespect he had shown for it. The article quoted a senior named Peter Tweig, who observed that the dean's outburst had breached Reed's honor principle. "I believe that *ad hominem* attacks of the sort employed by our Dean on Horowitz are fundamentally incompatible with the aims of a liberal education and the kind of dispassionate inquiry which it seeks to promote."

I could not have said it better myself. It reflected well on Reed, and it was precisely what the academic freedom campaign was about.[16]

THREE

Facing the Opposition

The opponents of the academic freedom movement—the faculty unions and the American Association of University Professors—have adopted an uncompromising stance, refusing to concede that a problem even exists. Is there a lack of diversity on university faculties? The first response invariably is that there is not. When the evidence of disparity becomes too substantial to deny, these critics respond that the disparity does not reflect purposeful exclusion and is ultimately unimportant; conservatives exclude themselves from faculties by choosing not to pursue academic careers but to make money instead.[1] (Tenured professors at elite schools like Princeton, it should be noted, make $160,000 a year for eight months' work and six hours a week in class. This remuneration hardly seems designed to discourage conservatives from seeking academic work.)

It has even been argued that the conservative view itself disqualifies one for an academic position because it indicates a lack of regard for evidence and an inability to reason. This point was actually made by Dean Steinberger—among many others—in an Internet exchange we had following our debate.[2] Steinberger wrote, "Remember: a relative absence of conservatives does not show that conservatives have been 'excluded.' Indeed, to the best of my knowledge, there has been no such exclusion. The large number of non-conservatives in (especially) elite institutions is almost certainly attributable not to any conscious or even unconscious regime of exclusion but to the simple fact that trained academics—strongly committed to notions of evidence and rational argument, hence innately hostile to claims based primarily on mere faith—are simply less likely to adopt conservative, especially socially conservative, viewpoints."[3]

Might inhabiting such a self-regarding (and self-affirming) universe encourage professors to vent their prejudices in unprofessional ways in the classroom? The response when this suggestion is made is: "What is the evidence?" Or, as one union official remarked, that the Academic Bill of Rights is "a solution in search of a problem."[4] If the evidence is then produced in the form of student testimonies, the response is: "This is mere anecdote and therefore meaningless."[5] Or, even, that proponents of the idea that there is such a problem are liars.[6] If students tape their professors to document the abuse, the response is: "This is snitching. It is McCarthyism." If a collective profile of professors who regard themselves as academic activists is produced with their own statements to that effect, the response is: "This book is a blacklist and its descriptions can't be trusted."[7]

The purpose of such attacks is not to engage an intellectual argument, but to suppress it. The same intransigence is seen in the fact that none of the opponents of the Academic Bill of Rights has offered to amend it. Instead, from the very outset, the opposition has taken the form of a no-holds-barred war, as tenured radicals are defending a political base they have established over the last few decades, which is perpetuated by their "right" to use academic classrooms for political agendas.

One early and influential "critique" of the campaign for academic freedom was written by Graham Larkin, a Stanford academic and a spokesman for the American Association of University Professors. Appearing in *InsideHigherEd.com,* Larkin's article bore the title "David Horowitz's War on Rational Discourse" and displayed the same incivility as Dean Steinberger but with even less grace:

> Enter L.A. tabloid editor David Horowitz, liar extraordinaire and author of the incomparable bullshitting manual *The Art of Political*

War and Other Radical Pursuits. This book, much applauded by Karl Rove, promulgates a political endgame in which brute force triumphs over any notions of intelligence, truth or fair play. The author contends that "you cannot cripple an opponent by outwitting him in a political debate. You can only do it by following Lenin's injunction: 'In political conflicts, the goal is not to refute your opponent's argument, but to wipe him from the face of the earth.'"[8]

Like Steinberger, Larkin invented his target, attributing to me Leninist sentiments that were not mine but that I had specifically described as the attitude of my opponents. As already noted, the advice I offered in *The Art of Political War* was not to follow Lenin or become a Leninist as Larkin accused me of doing. On the contrary, it was to prepare oneself for the Leninist attacks from the left, of which Larkin's article provided a pretty good example. Had Larkin quoted it, the full passage from *The Art of Political War* would have made this clear:

> The Democrats' destruction of Newt Gingrich was a classic example of successful political warfare. It had nothing to do with intellectual argument or political principle.[9] Nor could it. You can't cripple an opponent by outwitting him in a political debate. You can do it only by following Lenin's injunction: "In political conflicts, the goal is not to refute your opponent's argument, but to wipe him from the face of the earth." *Well, we needn't go as far as Lenin. After all, we're not Bolsheviks.* But destroying an opponent's effectiveness *is* a fairly common *Democratic practice.* Personal smears accomplish this. And *Democrats are very good at it.* Democrats invented sexual McCarthyism to destroy Robert Bork and Clarence Thomas. Democrats call their opponents mean-spirited and racist with precisely this end in view. If the voters think you are a bad person, they will not listen to what you have to say about anything at all.[10] [Emphases added.]

Well, we needn't go as far as Lenin. After all, we're not Bolsheviks. In other words, I wrote exactly the opposite of what Larkin claimed I had. Wiping an opponent from the face of the earth was not a strategy advocated by me. It was the strategy of *the*

Democrats towards Newt Gingrich, and also the strategy employed by Larkin and Steinberger in dealing with me: Don't even bother attempting to refute your opponent; destroy his credibility and eliminate him from the argument instead.

Again, I do not write this to settle a personal score. Conservative students and professors who inhabit the closed universe of the academy, which is politically dominated by the left and where such attacks can easily destroy a career, have suffered far worse and suffer for their views daily. Because the university is an institution the left regards as its political base, its rule of engagement is to take no prisoners.

Graham Larkin's attack was only the beginning. "Worse Than McCarthy" was the headline emblazoned on the essay page of the *Chronicle of Higher Education,* the leading journal of university affairs. This attack on the academic freedom campaign was authored by Professor Ellen Schrecker, a well-known university expert on the McCarthy era and a prominent figure in the radical left:

> Today's assault on the academy is more serious [than McCarthy's]. Unlike that of the McCarthy era, it reaches directly into the classroom. In the name of establishing intellectual diversity, Horowitz and his allies want to impose outside political controls over core educational functions like personnel decisions, curricula, and teaching methods. Such an intrusion not only endangers the faculty autonomy that traditionally protects academic freedom, but it also threatens the integrity of American higher education.[11]

Each of the claims that Schrecker made was demonstrably false, and a simple reading of the Academic Bill of Rights should have served to dispel them.[12] Far from intending to "impose outside political controls over . . . personnel decisions," the Academic Bill of Rights says in the clearest manner possible: "No faculty shall be hired or fired or denied promotion or tenure on the basis of his or her political or religious beliefs." Since Schrecker's accusation appeared three years after the original misrepresentations in the *Rocky Mountain News,* there is no possibility—no matter how careless a scholar she is—that she would not know this fact. I have referred to it on countless occasions in rebutting similar misrepresentations, including, as it happens, in an article that appeared two years earlier in the same *Chronicle of Higher Education*.[13] Schrecker's other charges are equally without foundation, since neither I nor the Academic Bill of Rights, nor any legislation associated with the academic freedom campaign, proposes "political controls over core educational functions like ... curricula, and teaching methods."

Schrecker is a tenured radical out to defend the political exploitation of the academy that she and her allies have engineered. Not surprisingly, the several books she has written on the McCarthy era serve political goals as well. All are written from a view sympathetic to the Communists and their political agendas. "I do not think that I conceal my sympathy for many of the men and women who suffered during the McCarthy era," Schrecker wrote in *Many Are the Crimes,* "nor my agreement with much (though not all) of their political agenda."[14] In an earlier work, Schrecker explained: "what made McCarthy a McCarthyite was not his bluster but his anti-Communist mission...."[15] In other words, it was not McCarthy's tactics or lack of ethics that was the problem; it was his opposition to Communism.

Schrecker's antipathy to opponents of Communism and her support for politics that are only slightly separated from those of the Communists themselves provide the only credible clues to understanding how she could confuse the Academic Bill of Rights, which protects all political viewpoints, with the agenda of Senator McCarthy, who was intent on removing Communists from university faculties. Or how she could regard the author of such a bill, who had himself defended the right of radicals like Ward Churchill to exercise their free speech rights, as "Worse Than McCarthy."[16]

Even more extreme, if that was possible, was the attack by Joan Wallach Scott, an endowed professor at Princeton's Institute for Advanced Study, a venue in which Albert Einstein once

held court. Scott's position as the head of the famous Committee A on Academic Freedom and Tenure of the American Association of University Professors made her the titular leader of the
opposition to the academic freedom campaign.[17] Going Schrecker
one better, Professor Scott compared the Academic Bill of Rights
in a single sentence to the crimes of Mao, Tojo, Mussolini, Stalin
and Hitler in testimony she gave before the Pennsylvania Committee on Academic Freedom: "[The Academic Bill of Rights]
recalls the kind of government intervention in the academy practiced by totalitarian governments. Historical examples are Japan,
China, Nazi Germany, fascist Italy and the Soviet Union. These
governments sought to control thought rather than permit a free
marketplace of ideas."[18]

Professor Scott's opposition to the Academic Bill of Rights
stems from the fact that her academic politics are rooted in the
traditions of the Communist left. Her father was a member of
the Communist-controlled New York Teachers Union and was
fired in the 1950s under the Fineberg Law, which required teachers to disclose whether they were Communists and—in a Catch-
22 clause—also made membership in the Party a cause for
termination.[19]

School authorities were able to identify the teachers they fired
as Communists because of an informant named Bella Dodd, the
teacher union's onetime legislative liaison. Dodd was willing to
cooperate with authorities because she herself had been purged
from the Party for refusing to give up her Catholic faith. Even
though Dodd was a good Communist in everything but her religious belief, the Party organized a show trial to expel her from its
ranks because of the political heresy involved in the matter of her
faith. The proceedings of her trial were filled with false accusations about her character, which were typical of such purges. Later
she lamented that none of her comrades had stepped forward to
defend her, despite the years of service she had given to them and
to the cause they shared. (Such Party trials were not uncommon.
The screenwriter Albert Maltz once confided to a friend that his

interrogation before the House Committee on Un-American Activities was a walk in the park compared with the Party trial that he himself had to endure at the hands of his comrades.)[20] Humiliated and abused at her own trial, Bella Dodd left the Party an embittered ex-comrade and vowed to take her revenge.[21]

Professor Scott suppresses all this history in her account of her father's case, which is as deceptive as the Communist Party's propaganda line was at the time. Scott conceals the fact that her father was actually a Communist, which is not a small deception since it meant that he was a member of a conspiratorial organization loyal to an enemy power.[22] Instead she pretends that her father was persecuted for his ideals. In her disingenuous telling, these ideals were inspired not by Marx and Stalin, but by Thomas Jefferson and the Bill of Rights:

> My father was a New York City high school teacher, suspended in 1951 (when I was 10) and fired in 1953 for refusing to cooperate first with a congressional committee, and then with the superintendent of schools, on their investigation into Communist activity among teachers. Although formally tenured according to the rules of the board of education, my father lost his job because, in that moment of the early Cold War, his refusal to discuss his political beliefs and affiliations was taken as evidence that he was a Communist and therefore unfit to teach. This despite the fact that he was a devoted fan of Thomas Jefferson, the Bill of Rights, and the Constitution. . . .[23]

Professor Scott's misrepresentation of her father's case more than fifty years after the fact reveals how deeply political her agenda is (and how questionable her scholarship). We all have fathers to deal with, but Professor Scott claims that her own interest in academic freedom began with his case: "In the tallying of losses he experienced in that period—his job, his pension,[24] his financial security, many colleagues he had once considered friends—none was so painful as the loss of his academic freedom. . . . I remember wondering why he cared so much about a principle that had failed to protect him from an arbitrary exercise of political power. . . ."

When the true facts of her father's case are restored, however, it is clear that this was not a matter of academic freedom
and the failure to protect the free expression of ideas. It was about
membership in a conspiratorial organization that controlled its
adherents' expressions of opinion and that had unacknowledged
ties to a hostile foreign power. Nor was her father's case about
"an arbitrary exercise of political power," as Professor Scott writes.
The law under which her father was questioned and fired was a
law duly enacted by the New York legislature. There were, indeed,
serious constitutional questions in the case, concerning an American citizen's right to belong to a secret totalitarian organization,
controlled by a foreign enemy, while teaching in a taxpayer-
funded school. But these are not the issues that Professor Scott,
deliberately confusing her father's Stalinist commitments with
"Jeffersonian" political principles, wants to address.

Professor Scott's radical agenda and not her concerns about
academic due process is the true source of her opposition to the
Academic Bill of Rights. Her desire is to *defend* the intrusion of
political agendas into the academic process—the correct agendas—not to keep them out. "We worry about the idea of neutrality promoted by supporters of the Academic Bill of Rights,"
Scott testified to the Pennsylvania Committee on Academic Freedom. "It would prohibit professors from expressing judgment
about material they teach as well as about matters not directly relevant to course material." This is a red herring. There is no pro-
hibition in the Academic Bill of Rights on professors expressing
judgment about material that is within the area of their expertise
or relevant to the courses they teach, nor to the expression of any
opinion at all, however offensive it might be, outside the classroom. Nor is the restriction on introducing controversial matter
unrelated to the course material a plot hatched by the Academic
Bill of Rights. It is, once again, the core principle of the "1940
Statement of Principles on Academic Freedom and Tenure" issued
by Professor Scott's own organization: "Teachers are entitled to
freedom in the classroom in discussing their subject, but they

should be careful not to introduce into their teaching controversial matter which has no relation to their subject." Yet Professor Scott opposes this basic tenet of academic freedom, without conceding that that is what she is doing.

Professor Scott's commitment to political intrusions into the academy is reflected in her membership in the organization "Historians Against the War," which has condemned the American "occupation" of Iraq. As a member of a professional association of historians who have taken a political stand, Professor Scott, in fact, regards her political activism as integral to her academic work. "As feminist and historian," she has written in her principal academic work, "my interest is in the operations of power—how it is constructed, what its effects are, how it changes. It follows that activism in the academy is both informed by that work and informs it."[25] In other words, the purpose of her teaching and scholarship is not the carefully nurtured intellectual growth of her students or the pursuit of intellectual knowledge, but her political "activism"—the validation and inculcation of her political doctrines. While she may see no difference between the vocations of politics and scholarship, her statement is a confession of her opposition to the core understanding of academic freedom as expressed in the canonical statements of the American Association of University Professors, for which she is a spokesperson.

As an academic radical, Professor Scott is also a staunch advocate of the Palestinian cause and its efforts to dismantle the state of Israel. At a rally to protest the Academic Bill of Rights, Scott referred to its supporters as "the pro-Sharon lobby," a reference to Israel's conservative prime minister. In her view, the Academic Bill of Rights was not really about academic rights but was a plot by Zionists to persecute faculty who defend the Palestinian cause. Under Professor Scott's leadership, the American Association of University Professors has concentrated its concerns about academic freedom quite narrowly on cases that affect her political allies. These include Tariq Ramadan, a Muslim academic and grandson of the founder of the Muslim Brotherhood, who was hired by Notre Dame but denied a visa by the State Department because of his connections with al-Qaeda, the Muslim Brotherhood, and other terrorist groups; and Professor Sami al-Arian, the North American head and chief fund-raiser for the terrorist group Palestinian Islamic Jihad. In May 2006, al-Arian filed a guilty plea and was ordered deported. In the same month, members of Tariq Ramadan's institute in Switzerland were arrested by Swiss police for plotting to shoot down an Israeli civilian airliner.[26]

In an interview with the AAUP magazine, *Academe,* in which she summarized the recent "threats to academic freedom," Scott called the "persecution" of al-Arian—who had been fired from his professorship following his indictment—the "gravest" concern her academic freedom committee faced.[27] In a lecture at Princeton on September 8, 2005, she again defended al-Arian and Ramadan, and went over the academic freedom cases taken up by her committee. A reporter present summarized her account: "Of the incidents the AAUP has tracked since 9/11, Scott said, all but one have been instigated by the pro-Israel bloc."[28]

Like other professional academic groups, the American Association of University Professors has undergone a political radicalization since the time it was a consistent defender of professional standards and academic freedom. Even as Scott was telling her Princeton audience about the Zionist plot against Ramadan and al-Arian, the AAUP was organizing a conference in Italy featuring at least seven and possibly as many as nine academic leaders of the campaign to boycott Israeli universities and professors (out of a total of twenty-one participants). Yet the campaign to boycott Israeli universities and professors was as direct an assault on academic freedom as one could imagine.

The scheduled AAUP conference imploded when an anti-Semitic article, "The Jewish War on Nazi Germany," was circulated to participants by the AAUP sponsors as part of the conference materials. The article was written by a Holocaust denier, prompting the Rockefeller Foundation and two other major funders to withdraw their support, which in turn caused the AAUP to "postpone" the event. The AAUP Executive Committee said that this was not as a matter of principle, but "out of concern for our reputation and our relationship with our funding agencies." In a letter to the editor of *InsideHigherEd.com,* Professor Scott blamed "lobbyists on behalf of the current Israeli regime (or fellow travelers of those lobbyists)" for the debacle. In other words, Scott's response was to argue that the cancellation of a conference tainted by Holocaust denial was itself the result of a Zionist plot.[29]

The point here is not simply to criticize Scott's attitude and behavior, though obviously she has a politically self-serving definition of "academic freedom." Nor is it to indicate the role that cliché from the Sixties—"the personal is political"—plays in her work and her professional activism. Rather, the point is that far from being a marginal individual in the academic profession, as one might expect given her attitudes and commitments, Scott is one of its leading figures, loaded with honors, a member of the academic elite. That such a crude ideologue should rise to such academic heights and be head of the AAUP committee that deals specifically with questions of academic freedom is testament to the dominant position occupied by academic radicals in these matters, while it also clarifies how leftists have made "academic freedom" into a worse than meaningless concept.

It is because they are activists who regard the university as a political battleground that Joan Scott and the leaders of the American Association of University Professors have been in the forefront of the opposition to the Academic Bill of Rights and the campaign to restore professional standards to university classrooms. In December 2003, the AAUP issued the first—and certainly the most influential—statement condemning the Academic Bill of Rights, describing it as "Orwellian"[!] and a "grave threat to fundamental principles of academic freedom."[30]

The statement contained distortions and misrepresentations of the bill that were to become the familiar arguments of its critics.

These included the false claims that the bill would replace academic standards by political standards (as I have noted, it proposes just the opposite) and that it would require universities "to establish 'a plurality of methodologies and perspectives' by appointing a professor of Nazi political philosophy, if that philosophy is not deemed a reasonable scholarly option within the discipline of political theory." This sentence seems like something of a Freudian slip considering the AAUP's subsequent sponsorship of papers by Holocaust deniers at their aborted anti-Israel conference. But it is also simply false. The Academic Bill of Rights does not require "balance" and specifically rejects opinion that is not scholarly (like Holocaust denial) and would require no such appointment.

The AAUP statement also included the following false claim, which has been repeated by innumerable critics (and refuted innumerable times): "[The Academic Bill of Rights] proclaims that all opinions are equally valid." It does no such thing. In promoting "intellectual diversity," however, the Academic Bill of Rights does challenge efforts by faculty radicals to impose a political orthodoxy on the nation's classrooms. In this way, it could be seen as a threat to the *political* agendas of the activist left. But in challenging such political orthodoxies, the Academic Bill of Rights does not attack *academic* viewpoints just because they happen to be leftist. It defends a diversity of academic views. More concretely, it upholds principles of academic freedom that have been in place for nearly a century. In opposing these principles, radicals put themselves in the difficult position of attacking academic guidelines they claim to observe, while defending the injustices that take place in many college classrooms.

As George Orwell long ago observed, the attack on freedom begins with an attack on language; opponents of academic freedom have raised linguistic abuse to an art form. Criticism of the academic left is reflexively labeled a "witch-hunt," while attempts to describe the agendas of faculty activists as inappropriate are attacked as a political "blacklist."[31] This lexicology is designed to discredit opponents by associating them with a tainted past. Ironically, this is precisely the transgression—McCarthyism—they claim to abhor.

One of the conveniences of employing guilt by association is that it obviates the need for an argument. As one professor explained in a newspaper column, the mere fact that I was a conservative produced in him "a sneaking suspicion that political partisanship—not academic freedom—is at the root of [Horowitz's] ideological battle and that Horowitz's proposal threatens to kill the academic freedom he insists it is protecting."[32] But if partisanship were my overriding concern, why would I not have proposed an affirmative action hiring program for political conservatives, who have clearly been excluded from the faculties dominated by the left? Why insert into the Academic Bill of Rights an explicit injunction *against* such a program? The only possible answer is that partisanship is not my overriding agenda. I am a *liberal* conservative who believes in due process and in the traditional mission of a democratic education. Most conservatives are "liberal" in this sense. Evidently many liberals are not.

FOUR

Indoctrination U.

In a democracy, the purpose of an education is to teach students *how* to think, not *what* to think—so goes the common wisdom. In the more formal phrasing of the 1915 "Declaration of Principles" on academic freedom, the purpose of a university education "is not to provide ... students with ready-made conclusions, but to train them to think for themselves, and to provide them access to those materials which they need if they are to think intelligently." In other words, a democratic education should not force-feed students opinions on controversial issues that teachers deem "politically correct." It should create citizens who are able to figure out what conclusions they wish to draw on their own. This is the idea that lies at the heart of the existing academic freedom provisions of virtually every university in America; the failure to observe these provisions is the crux of the educational crisis that the Academic Bill of Rights seeks to address.

The situation has been made possible because university administrators have increasingly abdicated their oversight of what faculty say and do on the job. With their attention focused on financial concerns, administrators have turned a blind eye to radical advocacy in the classroom and to the increasingly prevalent substitution of political posturing for scholarly discourse and research. As a result, academic standards have plummeted, while important segments of the faculty have become accustomed to engaging in conduct that is irresponsible and unprofessional, and have been able to do so without consequence, and therefore have come to regard such license as their academic right.

A second element of this crisis is the growing power of faculty radicals. This has led to the creation of academic programs that are overtly ideological in nature, and to agendas that are shaped by political rather than scholarly goals.[1] An advanced stage of this intellectual corruption is manifest in courses and even entire departments that are devoted to indoctrination in sectarian dogmas. To take one at random, a course in "Modern Marxist Theory," taught by Martha Gimenez at the University of Colorado and listed in the university catalogue as Sociology 5055, describes its curriculum in this way: "This seminar is designed to give students the ability to apply Marx's theoretical and methodological insights to the study of current topics of theoretical and political importance."[2] In other words, this is a course in how to be a Marxist. It is not—by its own description—an academic examination of Marxism that might also consider how Marxism has failed or why it might not provide "insights" into current topics of importance.

This anti-intellectual development in higher education is also manifest in the Women's Studies Department at the University of California, Santa Cruz, where faculty radicals have even changed the departmental name to reflect the ideological nature of its mission. It is now called the Department of Feminist Studies, and its curriculum represents an undisguised program of ideological indoctrination in the theory and practice of radical feminism.[3] This includes the recruitment of students to radical causes. Thus, the official departmental website lists "Career Opportunities" under the heading "What Can I Do with a Major in Feminist Studies," a question it answers as follows:

Employment Opportunities for Feminist Studies Majors
With a background in women's and minorities' histories and an understanding of racism, sexism, homophobia, classism, and other forms of oppression, graduates have a good background for work

with policy-making and lobbying organizations, research centers, trade and international associations, and unions. Graduates' knowledge about power relationships and injustice often leads them to choose careers in government and politics, because they are determined to use their skills to change the world. . . .[4]

This is not an academic curriculum; it is a party agenda. The Department of Feminist Studies at Santa Cruz is a training program for a radical cause that violates the fundamental principles of the academic profession in general and the University of California in particular.[5] Yet apparently, not a single state official or UC administrator is concerned.

"Peace studies" is an entire field—among several that could be mentioned—whose agenda is obviously not academic but political. In the case of peace studies, this agenda is antimilitary and anticapitalist. Among the more than 250 peace studies programs in America, for example, there does not appear to be one that includes on its faculty a professor of military science, although the sole rationale for the military in a democracy is to keep the peace. The point is not that this rationale for the military cannot or should not be challenged. It is that an academic course worthy of the name would need to confront such questions, not answer them in advance. The curricula of peace studies programs show beyond any reasonable doubt that the answers to questions concerning the role of the military have already been determined by the faculties that administer them, and that their specific agenda is to recruit students to the antimilitary left.[6]

Brett Mock, a political science major at Ball State University in Indiana, enrolled in its Peace Studies program with the idea that the curriculum would fill out his resumé for the political career he was planning. Mock did so even though he was a College Republican because the program was billed as an academic course in the causes of war and peace—"the study of methods of achieving peace within communities and among nations; history of peace movements and the causes of conflict; and analysis of principles to resolve conflict using case studies."

Once enrolled in the introductory class taught by the program's director, Professor George Wolfe, student Mock discovered to his dismay that the class was a recruitment and training course in left-wing politics and antimilitary attitudes. Without exception, the course lectures and texts guided him and his classmates to a view of America as an enemy of global peace, and to a sympathetic understanding of the terrorists who have attacked it. Among the "methods of achieving peace" recommended by Professor Wolfe was a menu of radical organizations that students were encouraged to join. These included PeaceWorkers, which is part of a coalition that includes the pro-terrorist Muslim Students Association and the Young Communist League, and for which Professor Wolfe is the campus adviser. Students who traveled to Washington to oppose America's efforts to topple Iraq's dictatorship were given academic credit for doing so; students who supported their country had no similar opportunity.

Not only is Professor Wolfe a political activist in the classroom, he is academically unqualified to teach this subject with its broad-ranging forays into history, geopolitics and global economics. Wolfe is a performance artist in the Department of Music at Ball State. His academic credential is a doctorate in education and his specific expertise is the saxophone. Apprised of these facts, the national campus director of Students for Academic Freedom sent a letter to the administration at Ball State expressing concern about the nature of the course and its failure to conform to educational standards.[7] The reply came from the provost and vice president for academic affairs, Beverley Pitts, who said that she had investigated Brett Mock's claims (without interviewing Mock) and concluded that they were mistaken. In particular, she wrote that the course met academic standards and was not one-sided; but she did not provide any evidence for her claim.

Addressing the issue of how a professor of the saxophone was academically qualified to teach the social, economic and cultural causes of war and peace, the provost wrote: "Dr. Wolfe has a doctorate in higher education from Indiana University; has received mediator training; is on the advisory board of the Toda Institute for Peace, Policy, and Global Research at the University of Hawaii; and has taught and published in the area of peace studies." Pitts did not explain how a doctorate in higher education would qualify Wolfe to head a program on the causes of war and peace, or how a training session in mediation techniques would do so either. The Toda Institute referred to in her letter, and on whose board Professor Wolfe serves as an adviser, is run by the Soka Gokkai, a Zen Buddhist pacifist cult.

Regarding Mock's complaint that the course involved indoctrination rather than a disinterested examination of the subject matter, Provost Pitts asserted: "Dr. Wolfe's class emphasizes critical thinking with respect to peace issues. The primary text for the class is Barash and Webel, *Peace and Conflict Studies* (Sage Publications, 2002), which presented various sides of peace- and war-related issues." Pitts' view of *Peace and Conflict Studies* would come as a surprise to its authors. In the preface to their book, Professors David Barash and Charles Webel write: "The field [of peace studies] differs from most other human sciences in that it is value-oriented, and unabashedly so. Accordingly we wish to be up front about our own values, which are frankly anti-war, anti-violence, anti-nuclear, anti-authoritarian, anti-establishment, pro-environment, pro-human rights, pro-social justice, pro-peace and politically progressive."[8]

In other words, the class text—*Peace and Conflict Studies*—makes no pretension to being an academic exploration of the complex issues of war and peace. It does not examine the different views of the problems that might lead to conflict, or the various assessments that might be made of the history of peace movements. It is, in fact, a left-wing manual whose purpose is to indoctrinate students in the radical view of the world shared by "progressives" like Noam Chomsky, Howard Zinn and Michael Moore. No indication is provided to the uninformed student that these might be extreme views, or that there might be other reasonable ways to look at these issues and events.

For example, *Peace and Conflict Studies* discusses the problems of poverty and hunger as causes of human conflict, but it approaches these issues exclusively through the eyes of Marxists such as Andre Gunder Frank and Frances Moore Lappe. The only academic credentials the authors themselves possess are in the fields of animal psychology (Barash) and philosophy (Webel). Nonetheless, their text is unhesitant in making bold pronouncements on these complex economic issues.

On the problem of global hunger, for example, the Barash-Webel text states: "To a very large extent, the problem of world hunger is not so much a production problem, so much as it is a *distribution* problem."[9] This is an easily recognized core doctrine of socialist economics, which has been discredited through the failed practices of Marxist regimes during the past century. The authors' claim would be news, for example, to the people of North Korea, where recent famine caused by their government's socialist policies killed more than a million people. It would be equally surprising to citizens of the former Soviet Union, whose Marxist leaders attempted to make equal distribution the center of their economic policy and wound up turning a country that had been the breadbasket of Europe into a nation of famines and chronic food shortages, until the collapse of the system seventy years later redirected attention towards production and restored some economic rationality to agricultural practice.

The *Peace and Conflict Studies* text relentlessly condemns the economic inequalities that characterize market systems, even though these systems are responsible for enormous agricultural surpluses and for raising billions of people out of poverty—facts the authors systematically ignore. Instead, they identify the culprits responsible for world poverty (and thus for the conflicts this suffering causes) in terms that would have pleased Lenin: "The greed of agribusiness shippers and brokers, plus control of land by a small elite leaves hundreds of millions of people hungry every day."[10] Students reading this with no critical texts for comparison might well conclude that it was reasonable for terrorists to hate rich countries like the United States.

Since the authors believe that the greed of the ruling class is responsible for world hunger, it is not surprising that *Peace and Conflict Studies* breaks its promise to readers to be "anti-violence" and does actually endorse one kind of violence, and one kind alone— the revolutionary kind. In the following passage, Barash and Webel explain how revolutionary violence can lead to good results:

> Consider the case of Cuba. In the aftermath of the Cuban Revolution of 1959, despite more than 40 years of an American embargo of Cuban imports and exports, infant mortality in Cuba has declined to the lowest in Latin America; life expectancy increased from 55 years in 1959 to 73 years in 1984; health care was nationalized and made available to all Cuban citizens at no or little cost; literacy exceeded 95%; and although prostitution, begging, and homelessness returned to Cuba in the 1990s (almost entirely for economic reasons due to the embargo and to the loss of support from the former Soviet Union), Cuba still has far fewer of these problems than virtually all other countries in Latin America. *While Cuba is far from an earthly paradise, and certain individual rights and civil liberties are not yet widely practiced, the case of Cuba indicates that violent revolutions can sometimes result in generally improved living conditions for many people.*[11] [Emphasis added.]

This is the extent of the analysis of Castro's dictatorship provided by the authors. No mention is made that Cuba is in fact a totalitarian system in which every citizen is a prisoner in his own country. No comment is offered on the fact that while Cubans can read, they can only read government-approved texts. No indication is given that Castro is the longest-surviving dictator in the world with a legendary record of sadism against his own supporters. The quality of care in Cuba's wretched medical system is not evaluated. Nor is the fact that in 1959, when Castro seized power, Cuba was the second-richest nation per capita in Latin America, but after nearly fifty years of socialism it ranks near the bottom of Latin America's twenty-two nations, above Haiti, but below Honduras and Belize.

When the authors do feel compelled to mention a deficiency in Cuba's achievement—whether political or economic—it is blamed on the United States and its embargo, even though Cuba trades with every other nation in the world and its economic woes are entirely attributable to the autocratic economic policies imposed by its dictator. This one-sided promotion of a Communist dictatorship is typical of the "scholarship" of this text and a representative sampling of the authors' ideological views. Throughout *Peace and Conflict Studies,* Professors Barash and Webel justify Communist policies and actions and put those of America and Western democracies in a negative light. In its account of the Cold War, *Peace and Conflict Studies* treats the Soviet Union as a sponsor of peace movements and the United States as the militaristic and imperialist power that peace movements—and thus students in the Peace Studies program—are supposed to keep in check.

Peace and Conflict Studies was written in 2001, and a brief section is devoted to the terrorist attacks of September 11. The authors begin by telling students that "Terrorism is a vexing term." It is vexing because from the "peace studies" perspective, the moral aspects of the term are purely relative: "Any actual or threatened attack against civilian noncombatants may be considered an act of 'terrorism.' In this sense, terrorism is as old as human history."[12] According to the authors, far from being an aggressive tactic—let alone criminal or evil—terrorism is a last resort of the weak, providing them with a means of self-defense: "'Terrorists' are people who may feel militarily unable to confront their perceived enemies directly and who accordingly use violence, or the threat of violence, against noncombatants to achieve their political aims." If one is weak, apparently it is all right to murder women and children if it advances one's cause.

According to Professors Barash and Webel, terrorism is also "a contemporary variant of what has been described as guerrilla warfare, dating back at least to the anti-colonialist and anti-imperialist struggles for national liberation conducted in North

America and Western Europe during the late 18th and early 19th centuries against the British and French Empires."[13] In other words, the American Founders were terrorists, and the terrorists in Iraq can be viewed as patriots.

In order that no one should miss this point, the authors of *Peace and Conflict Studies* explain: "Placing 'terrorist' in quotation marks may be jarring for some readers, who consider the designation self-evident. We do so, however, not to minimize the horror of such acts but to emphasize the value of qualifying righteous indignation by the recognition that often one person's 'terrorist' is another's 'freedom fighter.'"[14] The terrorists who killed three thousand innocent civilians from eighty countries in the heinous attacks of 9/11 can thus be viewed as "freedom fighters" striking at the oppressor because there are no other means available to them.

The *Peace and Conflict Studies* text continues: "After the attacks on the World Trade Center in New York City and the Pentagon in Washington, D.C., many Americans evidently agreed with pronouncements by many senior politicians that the United States was 'at war' with 'terrorism.' Yet, to many disemboweled [*sic*] people in other regions, 'Americans are the worst terrorists in the world' (according to Osama bin Laden in a 1998 TV interview with the American Broadcasting Company). Following the attacks, President George W. Bush announced that the United States 'would make no distinction between terrorists and the countries that harbor them.' For many frustrated, impoverished, infuriated people—who view the United States as a terrorist country—attacks on American civilians were justified in precisely this way: making no distinction between a 'terrorist state' and the citizens who aid and abet the state."[15] In other words, America is a terrorist state and the terrorists are liberators of the world's oppressed.

Peace and Conflict Studies is a widely used text in the more than 250 peace studies programs in America, which are generally similar in their extreme left views to the one at Ball State.

They teach students to identify with America's terrorist enemies and to identify America as a "Great Satan" oppressing the world's poor and causing them to go hungry. There are equally many provosts like Beverley Pitts (who has subsequently been appointed president of the University of Indianapolis) who are willing to defend—or turn a blind eye towards—the fraudulent academic practices that allow political activists to indoctrinate students in their political prejudices, notwithstanding the fact that they may be academically illiterate in the subjects they teach.

At the University of Texas, a world-class academic institution in other respects, a student can major in radical politics, although no such major is formally designated. This is because the courses are presented as courses in communications and rhetoric or as "studies" of African Americans or women. In these courses, students learn the history of radicalism from the point of view of radicals, and are schooled in the formal doctrines and propaganda techniques of the American left. This informal program is a joint project of several academic departments, which provide the umbrella for an academic major and include the Department of Communications Studies, the Center for Women's and Gender Studies, the Division of Rhetoric and Writing, the Centers for African and African American Studies, Mexican American Studies and Asian Studies.

An exemplary (and typical) course in this curriculum is "Communication and Social Change," taught by Professor Dana Cloud and offered by the Communications Studies Department. Professor Cloud has a university website that features a woman with a raised fist and a description of herself simply as "Activist."[16] She is a member of the International Socialist Organization, whose agenda, according to its website, is a Marxist revolution in the United States.[17] She describes her "course goals" in the university catalogue in these words:

CMS 340K—Course Goals:
The main purpose of this class is to encourage your engagement with the tradition and ongoing practice of movement for social

change in the United States. I believe this goal requires some history so that we can become familiar with the ways in which social change agents have used communication—from oratory to the internet—to raise awareness of injustice, demand redress, mobilize others in the cause, and prompt other kinds of direct action including civil disobedience and strikes. This historical knowledge is key to understanding the renaissance of social movements going on around us today—from the WTO to the University Staff Association. After the historical survey of social movements, the second part of the course asks you to become involved as an observer and/or as a participant in a local social movement. We will specifically address two prominent causes locally, the movement against the death penalty and the movement of University staff for higher wages and better treatment. We will also discuss some other current social movements including the fight against corporate globalization and the movement against sanctions in Iraq.

The guiding questions for the course are (1) How does social change happen? And (2) How can we use communication to intervene effectively and with integrity in the process of social change?[18]

There are only two required texts for the course, both written by Marxists (Howard Zinn and Robert Jensen). Like Cloud, these authors are sympathetic towards the radical Islamic cause. This lack of intellectual diversity reflects the ideological nature of the course and violates the principle of intellectual diversity which is crucial to the academic enterprise. If students are not exposed to a spectrum of views, they are being indoctrinated rather than educated. "Communication and Social Change" is not plausibly a course in communications theory, although it is a course offered in the Communications Studies Department.[19] Insofar as this course is about communications at all, it is a course in conducting propaganda for radical political movements.

The "Communication and Social Change" course is obviously designed to instill in students a radical political outlook, and then recruit them to join radical organizations (including, apparently, a staff union at the university). "Communication and Social Change" is not an appropriate course for an academic

institution, nor for an institution funded by the taxpayers of the state of Texas.

The university catalogue lists four other courses taught by Professor Cloud with identical political agendas, which raises several questions: How have Professor Cloud's unprofessional and overt political agendas passed unnoticed? How did a course like "Communication and Social Change" get departmental approval? Does the Department of Communications Studies have academic standards that would distinguish between an academic course and a course in political propaganda? Does the Liberal Arts faculty? Does the University of Texas?

These questions could be asked of university administrations and boards of regents in all fifty states. In the spring of 2006, I presented testimony including these concerns to legislative committees in Kansas and Pennsylvania.

I was invited by a Kansas legislator, Mary Pilcher Cook, to testify to the Appropriations Committee of the Kansas House of Representatives in March 2006, because of her interest in sponsoring a version of the Academic Bill of Rights. My remarks, with certain edits and emendations for readability and inclusion in this text, were as follows.[20]

What's the Matter with Kansas? is the title of a book by radical author Thomas Frank, which purports to show how the citizens of Kansas have been hoodwinked by conservatives into voting the Republican ticket against their interests. But if Kansas is a conservative state, as Frank maintains, its citizens have given over large areas of their state-supported educational system to agendas that are anything but conservative—or even academic. In overseeing Kansas's public universities, the Kansas Board of Regents has adopted policies to ensure that its educational system would be neither conservative nor liberal. Nonetheless, these policies have been extensively ignored.

Tenured faculty in Kansas schools—as elsewhere—are a privileged social and economic elite. The average full professor at the University of Kansas, which is not a particularly wealthy state, makes $92,253 a year and at Kansas State, $79,983, a figure well above the national mean. These are handsome payments for public officials, particularly since professors work an average of six to nine hours a week in class and are required to work only eight months out of the year. Virtually alone among workers in America, academics are entitled to four months paid vacation, and every seven years are awarded a sabbatical leave that provides them with ten months off at full or half pay. To crown these privileges, they alone among America's public employees—with the exception of Supreme Court justices—have lifetime jobs.

These great privileges are specifically granted by the Kansas Board of Regents—as they are by similar boards in other states— on the assumption that academics are professionals who work to acquire and then dispense an expertise that is of great benefit to society at large. The Kansas Board of Regents specifies these terms of its contract with professors in the following language: "It is the mastery teachers have of their subjects and their own scholarship that entitles them to their classrooms and to freedom in the presentation of their subjects."[21]

The contractual premise, then, is that professors are scholars who require prodigious amounts of time outside the classroom to conduct research that is scholarly and disinterested, and that encompasses such diligence and long years of effort as to render the results beneficial to society. This specialized diligence puts the intellectual work they do and conclusions they reach beyond the ken of laypersons who lack similar training and research experience, which is why the conclusions they reach *in their research* require academic freedom protections.

That is the contract. That is why university academics are paid more generously than most public employees, and why the elite among them are afforded lifetime tenure, a provision specifically intended to protect their valued expertise, not their inexpert opinions on controversial political and social matters.

"Academic freedom" and "academic tenure" are terms historically linked in all the policy statements concerning academic freedom by the American Association of University Professors and other academic agencies. Politicians and radio talk-show hosts do not have tenure or lifetime jobs. They do not have special freedom protections beyond what is guaranteed to all citizens through the First Amendment. That is because they deal in opinion, not specialized expertise.

In other words, the obverse side of the special privileges that professors enjoy is their obligation to be professional, to strive for scholarly objectivity, and to remain nonpartisan and nonpolitical in their classroom pronouncements. Professors are not granted tenure or the protections of academic freedom to defend their "free speech," which is already guaranteed to them as citizens by the First Amendment. They are granted these privileges to pursue their research wherever it might lead with the understanding that their classroom discourse will remain professional and expert.

According to the Kansas Board of Regents—and again this is a typical point in the academic boilerplate of collegiate institutions—being a professional requires a discipline not only within but also beyond the classroom:

> College and university teachers are citizens, members of a learned profession, and officers of an educational institution. When they speak or write as citizens, they should be free from institutional censorship or discipline, but their special position in the community imposes special obligations. As scholars and educational officers, they should remember that the public may judge their profession and their institution by their utterances. Hence, they should at all times be accurate, should exercise appropriate restraint, should show respect for the opinions of others, and should make every effort to indicate that they are not speaking for the institution. . . .[22]

Academic professionals are not alone in being expected to observe a discipline within the framework of an institutional mission. Military personnel, who risk their lives to defend all citizens' free speech, are nonetheless forbidden to express political views about the wars they are fighting. A pastor who goes into church on Sunday to preach a sermon that God does not exist will be looking for work on Monday, free speech rights or no. A nurse who interrupts an operation she is assisting to deliver a speech on nurses' salaries will probably not be invited into the same operating room again.[23] The rationale for these strictures is simple: the integrity and success of the mission require it. And simultaneously, the educational mission requires that professors deport themselves in a professional manner in the classroom. A professor who violates the standards of his profession will be (or ought to be) subject to disciplinary measures, including possible termination, for breach of contract.

While teachers are privileged with the freedom to express ideas that result from their expertise, they are required to limit their instruction to the areas of that expertise and not to inflict their prejudices—political or otherwise—on students in their classes. While teaching their expertise they are not permitted to fill their lessons with uninformed opinions they may hold as ordinary citizens or to vent their biases on controversial issues of the day, or to impose such attitudes on impressionable students through the authority they have been granted as a result of their expertise.

These strictures are made explicit by the Kansas Regents in a statement that draws on the AAUP's 1940 document: "Thus, it is improper for an instructor persistently to intrude material that has no relation to the subject or to fail to present the subject matter of the course as announced to the students and as approved by the faculty in their collective responsibility for the curriculum." And again: "Students should not be forced by the authority inherent in the instructional role to make particular personal choices as to political action or their own social behavior."

In other words, professors should not be indoctrinating students in feminism or any other ism. Nor should they be attempting to impose controversial positions or sectarian attitudes on students in their classrooms no matter what the subject.

Are these policies being violated in Kansas schools? There is no question but that they are. Entire departments at Kansas State and the University of Kansas are explicitly devoted to agendas that are ideological and political in nature, and not academic. They are advocacy programs designed to indoctrinate students in one-sided views of controversial issues, and therefore violate the mandates of the Kansas Board of Regents.

At Kansas State University, for example, the Women's Studies Program is described in the catalogue this way:[24]

> To qualify for a B.S. or B.A. degree in Women's Studies, students will have demonstrated:
> - Their understanding that Women's Studies is an academic discipline that generates new knowledge about women and gender, *reconsiders other disciplines through feminist perspectives, and is committed to social action and social change.*
> - Their familiarity with key Women's Studies concepts such as *the social construction of gender, oppression of and violence against women, heterosexism, racism, classism, and global inequality.*
> - Their understanding of *how and why gender inequality developed and is maintained in the United States and in our global society.*
> - Their ability to identify and apply a broad range of *feminist perspectives and theories to their personal experiences, professional work, and to their understanding of society.*[25]

This is not the mission statement of an academic program of scholarly inquiry into the history and condition of women; this is an ideological program frankly designed to school students in "feminist perspectives," to indoctrinate them in a radical feminist view of the world, and to recruit them to feminist causes. Thus the statement takes an explicitly sectarian (and therefore nonacademic) view of issues that are controversial—whether women are in fact "oppressed" in the United States, whether there is "gender inequality" in American society, or whether "heterosexism" and "classism" are meaningful let alone valuable categories of analysis. These are debatable issues, but apparently not in the Women's Studies Program at Kansas State.

On examination, the program is openly designed to recruit students to radical feminist causes and political agendas. Its core courses for establishing a major are not courses about women, but courses in the history, theory and practices of a particular ideology, namely radical feminism. The program is designed to be taught exclusively from the point of view of radical feminists, with assigned readings from texts by radical feminists. No intellectual diversity is contemplated. There is absolutely no justification for a program like this in an academic institution, let alone a taxpayer-funded one. Yet one could find a similar program at almost any public university in the country.

The academic program of the Women's Studies Department at the University of Kansas in Lawrence is designed with an identical framework. The syllabus of the introductory course required of all majors states: "Our focus is not only to look at how women are members of an oppressed group, but how women have always been active agents in changing the world in which they live."[26]

This is a program to implement a political agenda. An academic program, by contrast, would ask *whether* women are members of an "oppressed" group. It would not focus on the alleged fact that they are. This is a controversial claim that finds no unanimity in our political culture. An academic course would not place at its center the idea that its graduates should be "active agents in changing the world." These ambitions are political, not scholarly.

The mission statements and curricula of these two Kansas women's studies programs violate the standards set by the Kansas Board of Regents. Radical feminism is not an academic category or enterprise; it is a sectarian political movement. Professors who teach radical feminism are not scholars; they are political activists. This is why radical feminists do not permit intellectual critics like Camille Paglia and Christina Hoff Sommers to enter their programs. A bibliography for the course "Introduction to Women's

and Gender Studies" at the University of Texas lists a well-known
book by two conservative feminists, Daphne Patai and Noretta
Koertge, this way: "Daphne Patai and Noretta Koertge, *Professing Feminism,* passim (note that this represents ANTI-women's
studies—prepare to refute it)."[27] Real scholars would welcome
the diversity that Patai and Koertge represent, and would encourage their students to evaluate it. But activists fear criticism and
disdain contrarian viewpoints as complicating their agendas of
indoctrination and action.

On what basis should political activists in women's studies
departments be granted tenure and lifetime jobs? Professors of
women's studies at the University of Kansas are not elected. They
are appointed, and in fact they are self-appointed, since new hires
in the Department of Women's Studies will be determined by
the votes of the tenured members of the department. This means
that not only is there no intellectual diversity in women's studies programs now, but as long as ideological departments continue to exist there never will be. The tenured members of these
departments know the ideology they want in a hire, and will
always hire someone who believes politically as they do. An analogy would be if the Republican majority in the Kansas Legislature had lifetime jobs and were entrusted with electing their
Republican successors. This is a prescription for authoritarian
rule, not the kind of principle that should govern the educational
institutions of a democracy.

The women's studies programs at these schools are neither
small nor insignificant. At the University of Kansas, the Department of Women's Studies—which is, in practice, the Department of Feminist Ideology—lists more than thirty courses. How
did such a political enterprise, totally inappropriate for an academic institution and totally inappropriate for a state institution,
get funded in the first place? How is it that no one in the administration of either of these two universities noticed that such advocacy programs violate the core policies of academic freedom that
have been established by the Kansas Board of Regents? Or, if

they did notice, how is it that they have allowed this massive misuse of public funds and abuse of Kansas students to take place?

Since the women's studies profession is organized nationally, and since women's studies professors are credentialed through a system that is also national, the departments at Santa Cruz, Kansas State and the University of Kansas are not (and cannot be) regarded as isolated circumstances, but reflect a general corruption of the women's studies field. Yet the lack of enforcement of academic standards has become so much the rule of academic life that there is almost no commentary addressed to this academic travesty, and as yet no remedial effort to correct it.[28]

Women's studies is not alone in exhibiting these problems. Dozens of fields have been corrupted in a similar manner. At Kansas State, the Social Work Program—to take but one arresting example—describes itself to students this way: "Social work is a profession for those with a spark of idealism, a belief in social justice, and a natural love of working with people."[29] The term "social justice" may seem a neutral term, but only for someone not familiar with the code of the radicalized academy. The phrase does not mean "justice for all" in the legal sense, but encompasses an "economic justice" that the free-market system allegedly denies and that the welfare state is required to redress. It is also a term that embraces racial and gender preferences, "living wage" and "equal pay" programs, and other "progressive" schemes. In other words, it is a partisan code for many of the most polarized political debates in our democracy. The Social Work Program at Kansas State, funded by taxpayers who are on either side of this debate, is training students to be partisans of only one side. This is hardly healthy for the democratic process; it certainly is not compatible with an academic program or with the principles of academic freedom.

Social Work 525 is one of the required courses for majors in social work at Kansas State. Its syllabus for students describes "Social Work's Core Values" and lists "social justice" as the second of these values:

Social Justice—*Social workers challenge social injustice.*
Social workers pursue social change, particularly with and on behalf
of vulnerable and oppressed individuals and groups of people. Social
workers' social change efforts are focused primarily on issues of
poverty, unemployment, discrimination, and other forms of social
injustice. These activities seek to promote sensitivity to and knowledge about oppression and cultural and ethnic diversity.[30]

Once again, this is the program of a political party or of a
training school for political party activists. It does not represent
an academic approach to social work. It is a program of radical
social activism, funded—no doubt unwittingly—by the taxpayers of Kansas.

The entire Social Work Program at Kansas State is, in fact,
an advocacy program for left-wing "solutions" to social problems. A left-wing point of view is a legitimate part of the political debate within our culture, but it is only one point of view,
and constitutes only one side of the argument. A Kansas State
student who does not accept the premises and goals of the radical Social Work Program will fail the program, because he or
she will be unable to "understand" its core beliefs. More likely,
such a student will never be admitted to the program in the first
place, no matter how much he or she wants to help poor people. This is not an academic program. It is an ideological and partisan agenda, and it violates the academic freedom policies of the
Kansas Board of Regents.

Social Work 510 and Sociology 510 constitute a joint course
titled "Social Welfare As a Social Institution," which is taught
under the jurisdiction of both the Social Work Program and the
Sociology Department at Kansas State. Social Work 510 is an
especially egregious example of political indoctrination masquerading as academic discourse. Its syllabus explains the course
agenda: "An understanding of the development of social injustice is a necessary first step toward working for social justice."[31]
This is a statement of advocacy, not a program of inquiry.

Both required texts for Social Work 510 were written by political ideologues, and are political rather than scholarly treatises. The first is titled *A New History of Social Welfare,* by Phyllis Day. Currently in its fifth edition, this text views America as a racist society.[32] The author explains to students that "Institutional discrimination permeates American systems so deeply that we may not recognize it. Based on hostile attitudes reified in rules, regulations, and procedures, its forms—racism, sexism, ageism, homophobia or heterosexism, and 'otherism'—deny equal rights and opportunities even when no individual prejudice may be involved."

The author of these statements does not bother to explain how such institutionalized discrimination is possible in light of the Fourteenth Amendment guarantee of equal treatment under the law or in light of antidiscrimination laws on the books, nor does she explain how racism can exist in the absence of "individual prejudice." But she does make clear that only white people can be racists: "Racism is prejudice with power *against people of color:* African Americans, Hispanics, Asian Americans and Native Americans." (Emphasis added.) Moreover, *A New History of Social Welfare* ascribes the existence of racism to American values: "Our American values make us assume that race determines human traits and capacities and that white people are inherently superior to people of color."[33]

The perspective of *A New History of Social Welfare* is well to the left of the Democratic Party. The text makes extensive attacks on American welfare legislation authored by both parties, and sums up its radical point of view on these matters in its concluding pages, which begin: "The 104th Congress and Presidents Bush, Clinton, and G. W. Bush legitimized control by the wealthy in the legislative, judicial and administrative branches of government, undercutting the promises of the nation for equal opportunity and equal treatment under the law. In addition, they have reinvested patriarchy—control of women, children, and workers—with a new 'morality' that defies humankind's vision of social morality."[34]

The main text for the Social Work 510 course, however, is not even a text in social welfare policy. Instead, it is a well-known Marxist indictment of American history from Christopher Columbus to the present, written by Howard Zinn. As the online syllabus makes clear, Social Work 510 is virtually a chapter-by-chapter, class-by-class reading of Zinn's political tract, *A People's History of the United States.*

Howard Zinn is a well-known radical who supported the Soviet empire during the Cold War, and whose book describes America as a repressive and predatory capitalist state—sexist, racist, imperialist—that is run by a corporate ruling class for the benefit of the rich. According to Zinn, the root causes of social injustice are private property and private corporations, the very foundations of America's legal, political and business systems. According to Zinn, America is the world's "greatest terrorist state," and the terrorists that America faces are victims of American imperialism and oppression and thus are "freedom fighters." Furthermore, in Zinn's view the entire American system of government and its laws should be overthrown and replaced with a socialist system.

At its best, *A People's History of the United States* is neither a sociology text nor a text about social welfare institutions, but a work of popular history. What is the expertise of a professor of social work that he or she would be qualified to evaluate this text or to teach the history of the United States from Columbus to the Vietnam War? More to the point, what is the relevance of this history to the training of Kansas State students for careers in social work? Obviously, there is none. This is a course designed to indoctrinate students into a left-wing worldview.

How can this course be justified under the rules laid down by the Kansas Regents? The question is rhetorical: it cannot. Social Work 510 is a course in the evils of American capitalism, taught by amateurs who lack any professional credential for teaching the subject and whose only agenda is to impose their political prejudices on impressionable students. But there is apparently no one in the Kansas State administration who is interested in looking into these matters, which are central to the maintenance of academic integrity and academic standards.

Social Work 510 violates every tenet of Kansas State University's existing academic freedom policies, yet according to the catalogue it has been offered since 2001. It is designed to immerse students in a Marxist view of American history, which proposes the destruction of the very system in which students are supposedly seeking to improve themselves by eventually gaining employment as social workers. No society can survive if its schools become one-sided indoctrination centers in propaganda against it. But this is just one such course among many at Kansas State.

My testimony in Kansas took place on March 15, 2006. Three months earlier, I had appeared as the final witness before the Pennsylvania Committee on Academic Freedom, which met at Temple University, one of three large public universities in the state.[35] Temple's academic freedom policy, along with those of other public universities in Pennsylvania, is the "1940 Statement of Principles on Academic Freedom and Tenure" of the American Association of University Professors. The statement says that "teachers are entitled to freedom in the classroom in discussing their subject, but they should be careful not to introduce into their teaching controversial matter which has no relation to their subject."

Temple is typical of Pennsylvania schools in that it does not enforce its own academic freedom policy and does not inform students of their academic freedom rights under the policy. Consequently, the injunction against introducing controversial matter irrelevant to the subject is routinely and at times egregiously violated, not only at Temple but at every campus in the state of Pennsylvania.[36]

The following testimony was offered at the Pennsylvania hearings by Temple student Logan Fisher, president of the College

Republicans: "The Chairman of the History Department, who is my adviser, told me during advising that 'If Bush gets re-elected we will have a fascist country.' He [told me] he will be scared for his survival and will consider possibly moving to Canada. That's scary coming from a history professor."

It is also unprofessional. This student had come to his adviser's office for a "graduation review," that is, for advice on the courses he needed to complete his major. What academic or counseling purpose could be served by this professor's venting of his political anxieties to a student he knew to be a Republican, or to any student, for that matter? Logan Fisher also testified, "All the professors had Kerry [election] signs on their [office] doors. . . . Every single door to the offices, all the professors had a Kerry sign. . . . We also have 'God Is Not a Republican' signs all over campus."[37]

State universities in Pennsylvania spend tens of millions of dollars every year to inform their students that sexual and racial diversity are fundamental university values and that harassment on the basis of gender and race will not be tolerated. They provide elaborate grievance machinery to deal specifically with these issues. They insert these values, along with guides to the grievance process, into freshman orientation sessions; they put them into student handbooks; and they distribute literature to inform students about them. But these same universities do not spend a single penny on promoting the values of intellectual pluralism and academic freedom, which the American Council on Education has judged to be "central principles of an American higher education"[38]

It is not only students who are in the dark about their rights. One of the administrative witnesses at the Pennsylvania hearings was Professor Burrell Brown, chairman of the Department of Business and Economics at California University, which is part of the Pennsylvania State system. Professor Brown testified that a statement contained in the Pennsylvania House bill (HR 177) authorizing the hearings was a problem for him. The bill stated that professors should not persistently introduce into their classrooms controversial matter that has no relation to the subject. Professor Brown responded, "The questionable part of House Resolution 177 is that it specifies that faculty may not introduce controversial subjects when they're inappropriate, but it gives no mechanism or means for determining who gets to say what is controversial."[39]

Professor Brown was evidently unaware that the statement about not introducing controversial matter irrelevant to the subject was quoted verbatim from a famous academic freedom statement,[40] or that it was the official policy of all public universities in the state of Pennsylvania, including his own.[41] Professor Brown discussed his presentation with the president of his university before testifying, which suggests that his ignorance of the academic freedom principle of his own university is not merely a personal lacuna. Since no administrator in the Penn State system commented (or acted) on the numerous violations of this principle during the 2004 presidential election or the war in Iraq, it is probable that this ignorance is widespread. It is further possible that prior to the academic freedom hearings virtually no one in the Pennsylvania State system was aware that professors had a responsibility not to inflict on their students controversial opinions that had no relation to their subjects.

The following student complaint about an English literature course at Temple was posted on the Internet bulletin board sponsored by Students for Academic Freedom:[42]

> This professor always had something negative to say not only about the Bush Administration, but about conservatives in general. She stated on one occasion that it is impossible to be a moral capitalist. She stated that the US does not have the right to say anything about the Taliban's record of oppressing women because the US oppresses women too.... I began to feel physically sick from her misrepresentation of facts, and on numerous occasions I stood up to her and tried to advocate my opinion. She'd cut me off in mid-argument....

Incidents like this don't take place unless there is a university culture supporting them. That is why academic freedom policies protecting students from political indoctrination have to be stated and codified, and ultimately enforced as student rights. Unless the administrations at Temple and other Pennsylvania universities show they are ready to do so, the responsibility must fall to the legislature, which funds these institutions, to see that the principles are honored.

The legislation creating the Pennsylvania hearings states that "Academic freedom is likely to thrive in an environment of intellectual diversity...." But Temple University's policy does not include a statement about intellectual diversity, and its academic programs regularly violate the principle. For instance, Temple provides a "writing-intensive two-course sequence" called "Intellectual Heritage" which is required of all Temple students, and which includes, among other subjects, a focus on Enlightenment, Romantic and Revolutionary Thinkers. The Revolutionary Thinkers include Darwin, Marx and Freud, but not Adam Smith, the thinker most associated with the system in which Temple students live. Professors involved in the course have posted guides for students on a department webpage, which has a section called "Faculty Perspectives on Marx."[43] Virtually all the faculty guides provided in this section are explications of Marx's writings, without critical comment.

On the Temple webpage, I counted about thirty sample exam and study questions provided by the professors in the program relating to Marx. Every one of them prompts students to explain what Marx said in the way you would expect students to explain the theories of a scientist like Isaac Newton, whose hypotheses have been proved by real-world experiments.

Here is a sample guideline suggested by one Intellectual Heritage professor: "Marx presents an astute understanding and critique of Capitalism. Is it convincing?" The question does not say, "Marx analyzed capitalism. Is his analysis convincing?" There is no indication in the guide that there might be grounds for thinking that it is not convincing, while the professor has already informed the student that he thinks Marx's analysis is "astute."

Consequently, the "question" put by the teacher is more an assertion in disguise, in that it tells the student what to think: Marx wrote a wise critique of capitalism. Are you persuaded? What if you are not persuaded or do not think it wise, and suppose you encountered this question on an exam. Are you going to contradict your professor and risk a possible repercussion to your grade? This is not education; it is indoctrination.

Not one of the faculty-provided guide questions asks students to consider that *all* economies run by Marxists—without exception—have failed, and have failed catastrophically. No mention is made of the fact that Marxist regimes have caused the immiseration of billions of people. They have produced man-made famines and human suffering on a historically unprecedented scale. Not one professor contributing to the Temple Intellectual Heritage webpage bothered to mention this. Not one.

The faculty treatments of Marx on the Intellectual Heritage webpage lack the essential ingredient of an academic inquiry—a consideration of alternative points of view. No critical literature on Marx and Marxism is offered. There is no confrontation with the most serious question that a thinker like Marx poses, since his ideas have had vast and immensely destructive consequences: namely, did these ideas lead directly to the murder of 120 million human beings and the poverty of billions? A comparable instruction would be to assign students *Mein Kampf* and provide a guide that doesn't mention the gas chambers or the Second World War. Judging from the Intellectual Heritage webpages, Temple students are not even aware that such questions need to be asked with respect to Marx, nor is there any indication that the answers might be devastating to the idea that Marx had "an astute understanding" of capitalism or anything else. This is not education; it is indoctrination.

The Intellectual Heritage Program is not the only Temple sequence that fails to observe basic academic guidelines. The First-Year Writing Program describes itself as having been designed "to provide Temple students with a comprehensive experience of writing to learn and learning to write." Because it is intended as a course to teach students the basics of English composition, the First-Year Writing Program is taught by the English Department. This one-year course is covered by "English 40" and "English 50" and is taught mainly by graduate students in English, whose evolving professional expertise is the English language and literature.

However, the "writing to learn" part of the First-Year Writing Program also has an ideological agenda that has nothing to do with expertise in the English language. Its themes are race and gender, and its approved texts are ideological, with a clear agenda of articulating the views on race and gender held by radicals in general and by radical feminists and race theorists in particular, even though some allowance is made for other views.[44] From the perspective of academic freedom, there are two things obviously wrong with this course.

The first is that it is unprofessional. English teachers are not experts in the sociology or history of gender or race. The official course handbook for the English composition sequence candidly acknowledges the complexity of its subject: "We will be using gender [and gender roles in American culture] ... because it is both relatively simple (everybody has one) and extremely complex in terms of how gender impacts people's lives and identities, feelings, and behaviors." But if this is an extremely complex subject, why is it being taught by youthful amateurs who have no professional training in the subject, and why do the readings overwhelmingly reflect one side of these controversial issues?

If the subject is writing for freshmen and the task is to teach students how to write, the class texts should properly be composed of writers who know how to write correctly, not writers picked for their "correct" political views on gender and race. Professionalism is at the heart of the academic freedom issue. When English instructors pontificate on the sociology of gender or race they are merely sharing their ignorance and uninformed prejudice, not their academic expertise.

If a department at Temple taught exclusively from a "German perspective" that Germans were a global community bound by blood and Germany was the center of world history, what would be the reaction? Suppose that there were a German American Studies Department at Temple that had an introductory course required of all majors, which stated its teaching philosophy in these words:

> As Aryan people, our strengths are found in the creation of communities. Whether these communities are on Broad and Erie [in Philadelphia], in Mesopotamia, on South Street or the classroom, we are building Aryan communities. *Our energy, spirit and blood bond us as an Aryan community.* As an Aryan community, during this course, we will engage many topics that will aid us in the further liberation of Aryan people. The goal, first and foremost, is to *allow* these experiences to contribute in our growth and development as Aryan people. The classroom is the community, the reading materials are our map, and Aryan consciousness is our guide. Let us continue the process of Aryan liberation!

Of course, Temple has no German American Studies Department. The paragraph quoted, except for the word "Aryan," is verbatim the stated "teaching philosophy" of the introductory course in "Afrikan American Studies" at Temple University. The statement actually reads: "We are building Afrikan communities . . . the reading materials are our map, and Afrikan consciousness is our guide. Let us continue the process of Afrikan liberation!"[45]

This is the program of a political and racial movement (replete with the old spelling of "African"), not the description of a course of academic study, which would necessarily include different and conflicting perspectives on Africa and on the descendants of Africans. Forging a blood community across continents and historical epochs is not an academic or scholarly enterprise and has no place in an institution of higher learning, particularly one funded by the taxpayers of Pennsylvania.

The Department of African American Studies at Temple has long been notorious for its ideological narrowness, its racism, and its lack of credible scholarship—all present from the moment it was conceived as a department. But it has always been protected by the Temple administration, fearful of applying credible academic standards to this racial fiefdom. Several books have been written about the travesty of Temple's African American Studies Department by eminent classical scholars from across the political spectrum. These books have demonstrated the fraudulent nature of its scholarship and of its central doctrine of "Afrocentricity," which has been exposed as a racist idea based on made-up history. The most famous of these authorities, Mary Lefkowitz, the Andrew W. Mellon Professor in the Humanities, emeritus, at Wellesley College, was instrumental in bringing women into the leadership of the American Philological Association, the professional association of classical scholars and ancient historians in the United States.

In her book *Not Out of Africa,* Lefkowitz characterizes "Afrocentricty" as the teaching of "myths disguised as history." Professor Lefkowitz's summary of these myths is as follows:

> There is little or no historical substance to many of the Afrocentrists' most striking claims about the ancient world. There is no evidence that Socrates, Hannibal, and Cleopatra had African ancestors. There is no archaeological data to support the notion that Egyptians migrated to Greece during the second millennium B.C. (or before that). There is no reason to think that Greek religious practices originated in Egypt. ... Other assertions are not merely unscientific; they are false. Democritus could not have copied his philosophy from books stolen from Egypt by Anaxarchus, because he had died many years before Alexander's invasion [of Egypt]. Aristotle could not have stolen his philosophy from books in the library at Alexandria, because the library was not built until [fifty years] after his death. There never was such a thing as an Egyptian Mystery System (which is a central part of Afrocentrist teaching).[46]

The curriculum of the African American Studies Department at Temple does not merely feature a course in Afrocentric theory. By its own account, this department is devoted to promulgating Afrocentric theory, its mythologies, falsehoods and racist ideas, and credentialing the next generation of professors to spread its cult to other schools. This is not intellectual diversity and it is not education; it is indoctrination.

The professor unions and the American Association of University Professors orchestrated an opposition to the Pennsylvania hearings. It started with the legislation authorizing the hearings themselves, which passed with only a handful of Democrats and Republicans crossing party lines. Coached by the teacher unions, Democrats opposed the bill as an attack on academic freedom rather than what it actually was, an attempt to restore academic standards and intellectual pluralism to Pennsylvania schools. After the hearings bill passed, the Democrats continued their attempts to sabotage the committee. At the very first session in Harrisburg, attorney David French testified that speech codes at fifteen of the seventeen universities in the Penn State system were violating their students' First Amendment rights. French was in a position to know since he had already successfully sued one of the Penn State campuses over the constitutionality of its codes. Yet after hearing this testimony, Representative Dan Surra, a Democrat member of the committee, attacked the proceedings as "a colossal waste of time." Afterwards, he told a reporter that it was "a hunt for Bigfoot."[47] There could be no clearer indication that the opposition was uninterested in the facts or in the academic freedom of Pennsylvania students.

Surra had little to fear in making such irresponsible comments, since a politically sympathetic press provided an echo chamber for opponents of the hearings. For example, the editors of the *Centre Daily Times,* the paper of record for the Penn State community, ran this editorial on the hearings, titled "Good Night, Good Luck," after the anti-McCarthy Hollywood film of the same name:

> Some might find irony in the timing; others could experience an eerie sensation that life and art, indeed, take turns imitating each

other, or that the Red Scare days of the post–Russian Revolution and the Cold War periods are back. George Clooney's film "Good Night, and Good Luck," which portrays television journalism icon Edward R. Murrow opposing Joseph McCarthy's attacks against anyone the senator could paint with a broad, pink brush, is playing at a theater near you. Meanwhile, state legislators of a true-blue conservative tint are holding hearings on academic freedom at state-supported universities.[48]

Although hearings had already been held in Harrisburg and at the University of Pittsburgh, the *Times'* editorial had nothing to say about what had actually taken place. And for good reason. The stated policy of the committee was that no names of individual professors or administrators were to be used by witnesses or committee members. The hearings were entirely about existing academic freedom policies and whether or not they were enforced. They had no conceivable relation to the McCarthy hearings, except in the minds of those who were looking for a club—any club—with which to batter those concerned about the state of academic freedom in Pennsylvania schools.

After the initial hearings and just prior to those at Temple and Millersburg, the Democratic co-chair of the committee, state representative Lawrence Curry, appeared as a featured speaker at two separate union rallies sponsored by the American Association of University Professors and the American Federation of Teachers. With Curry's approval, professor-activists mounted the podium to liken the hearings to a McCarthy witch-hunt. It was just another demonstration of the anti-intellectual hardball that characterized the opposition to the academic freedom campaign.

FIVE

Dangerous Professors

In the winter of 2006, the campaign for academic freedom was complicated by the publication of a book I had written called *The Professors: The 101 Most Dangerous Academics in America*. The appearance of this book ignited an even more ferocious opposition than was already the case. Many of the academics discussed in the book were interviewed by politically sympathetic journalists who were intent on ridiculing the notion that a professor might be "dangerous."[1]

To be fair, the subtitle of the book was a provocation and the response somewhat predictable, even though "dangerous" was not a claim actually made in the book. The subtitle was added to my original title by the publisher long after I had finished the manuscript. The text I wrote under the title I chose—simply *The Professors*—was a collective profile of political activists masquerading as scholars. In the selection of individuals for inclusion, the idea that they were "dangerous" had played no part.

There was an element of truth in the description, however. The academics were all ideologues of the left, which meant their growing influence in the academy would undoubtedly influence, in a negative way, America's war on terror. The claim that they might be the "*most* dangerous," on the other hand, was hard to justify. Because my intention was not to show extremes, but to reveal a pattern of professorial behavior that was widespread, there were obscure academics such as Marc Becker of Truman State and moderate leftists like Todd Gitlin. The inclusion of these two (and a few others) under the rubric "most dangerous" was bound to raise eyebrows, and legitimately so. This was of particular concern to me because I knew that my critics would jump on the word "dangerous" to avoid engagement with the issues raised in the book and to charge that it was a "witch-hunt."

I therefore opposed the addition of the subtitle when the publisher presented it to me. "If we give it this subtitle" I said, "academics will regard it as a witch-hunt and no one in the academy will read it." My publisher replied, "Who in the academy is going to read it anyway? They'll hate this book no matter what you call it and only ten of them will buy it, whatever its title. We need to market it to a large audience, and this subtitle will do the trick, and that's what we're going to do."

Journalists don't write the headlines of their articles, and most book authors aren't given the authority over their book titles. Moreover, the campaign to taint me with the McCarthy brush was already extensive, with more than a hundred thousand references on the Web. If two hundred tenured radicals at Harvard could censure its liberal president as a threat to the self-esteem of little girls and force him to resign, why would I think they could not discredit me, or discourage academics from reading my book? The major professional associations had already excoriated my campaign and attacked my credibility.[2] As both a writer and an academic reformer I could expect little support from media that academics respected—among them public radio and television, the *New York Times,* the *New York Review of Books,* the *Chronicle of Higher Education* and *InsiderHigherEd.com.* This adverse environment was entirely a response to my political views, and something I had become accustomed to as a writer. The books I had written when I was part of the left were regularly and positively reviewed in the same venues, and had made me a nationally known and respected author. But when my political views changed, my literary reputation changed as well. The last book of mine reviewed by the *New York Review of Books,* for example, was published in 1985, just prior to my becoming a conservative, and this was typical. I was a tainted figure, stigmatized in the liberal culture for my political views.

These facts disposed me to be somewhat fatalistic. If my political opponents could twist the details of the Academic Bill of Rights and turn them into their opposite, why should I think they would have any difficulty doing the same with this book, whatever its title? So I went along with the marketing strategy, which seemed to work. In its first six months of publication, *The Professors* sold thirty-five thousand copies and stimulated a national dialogue on the issues it was attempting to raise. But the strategy also facilitated the predictable attacks. Its political opponents were able to draw on the image of professors as absentminded and ineffectual to feign incredulity at its thesis: What, *me* dangerous?[3]

The main attack, of course, was the ludicrous idea that the book was a "witch-hunt." The teacher unions immediately denounced it as a reprise of Senator McCarthy's infamous roster of Communists in the State Department. Lists compiled from profiles in the book sprouted on left-wing websites, along with complaints from professors I had included.[4] Lengthy "reports" purporting to analyze the text and find it unrespectable were published on *MediaMatters* and other attack sites. *Academe,* a webzine of the Illinois Association of University Professors, posted complaints from more than twenty of the individuals featured. The idea seemed to be that if enough charges were directed at me, whatever their merits, I might suffer the death of a thousand cuts.[5]

Because Senator McCarthy kept changing his numbers, the opposition feebly tried to create a parallel impression that I'd done the same thing. They suggested that although my "list" *claimed* 101 names, there were really only 100.[6] In fact, the book did not purport to name members of a subversive organization (as McCarthy had), and the number of professors included could have been greatly expanded (as I explained in the text). The purpose of the profiles was not to assemble a definitive list but to draw the collective portrait of a professorial type—academics who were political activists rather than scholars, and whom I estimated to be representative of far greater numbers than I was able to include.

The only rationale for this kind of complaint was to insinuate the familiar parallel with McCarthy and to promote the idea that I was careless with facts. Because the main agenda was to discredit me as a witness and avoid dealing with the issue, the allegation that the book's profiles were inaccurate was the principle theme of the attacks. This culminated in a fifty-page "report" called "Facts Count," which was compiled by an organization specially created by the teacher unions for this purpose—the Coalition for a Free Exchange of Ideas on Campus.[7] An article about the Free Exchange report titled "Fact-Checking Horowitz" appeared on *InsideHigherEd.com*.[8] The Free Exchange coalition created an entire website to discredit me, featuring a section pointedly called "Horowitz Fact-Checker" (which is where *InsideHigherEd.com* picked up its title).

Both "Horowitz Fact-Checker" and the "Facts Count" report were poorly conceived and transparently tendentious. Their accounts of what I said were filled with inaccuracies and errors; they imputed to me things I had not said and held me accountable when I failed to provide evidence to substantiate the claims they had invented; they repeated misrepresentations of what I had written that I had already refuted when others reported them. They confused differences of opinion with factual accuracy, claiming I "lied" when I simply disagreed with their interpretations. And they inflated small mistakes—normal to any printed work—into substantive errors.[9]

Like the Academic Bill of Rights, *The Professors* was not about "un-American" ideas or subversive affiliations. Nor was it about removing the proponents of left-wing ideas from university faculties. The introduction made this inescapably clear: "Every individual, whether conservative or liberal, has a perspective and therefore a bias. Professors have every right to interpret the subjects they teach according to their individual points of view. That is the essence of academic freedom."[10]

The Professors was about an academic minority I estimated to be at 10 percent of a given faculty, who regarded political activism as their academic mission.[11] This was not a small number in absolute terms, as it translated into more than fifty thousand professors nationally, concentrated overwhelmingly in the humanities and social sciences.[12] "As tenured radicals," I had written, these academics "rejected the idea of the university as a temple of the intellect in which the term 'academic' described a curriculum insulated from the political passions of the times. Instead, they were intent on making the university 'relevant' to current problems and events and to their own partisan agendas. Accordingly, they set about reshaping the university curriculum to support their political interests, which appeared grandiosely in their own minds as crusades for 'social justice.'"[13]

Seven weeks after *The Professors* was published, I arrived at Duke University to give a speech on these questions. More than six hundred students attended the event, televised by C-SPAN, and were overwhelmingly polite and responsive. But the proceedings were periodically interrupted by a band of protesters made up entirely of women and roughly thirty in number, who giggled on cue at intervals throughout my remarks. The protesters, as I later discovered, were organized by three faculty members including the director of undergraduate studies for the Anthropology Department, a tenured radical named Diane Nelson.

All the demonstrators wore black anti-Horowitz T-shirts provided to them by Nelson and the Anthropology Department. The shirts featured adolescent political messages emblazoned in white lettering: "Why Didn't I Make the List?" and "Narcing on Professors = Academic Freedom?"[14] The following day, the *Duke Chronicle* published a memo that Professor Nelson had written and then sent through the university e-mail system urging students to protest my speech and suggesting that they strip to the waist as part of her plan to obstruct it.

Nelson's proposal to students to perform a strip-tease had no takers, but the interruptions were disruptive. At one point in the proceedings, a student in the audience announced that he was a leftist and did not want to be associated with the embarrassing antics of the group. That drew enough applause to dampen the enthusiasm of the protesters, while not entirely discouraging their displays. My remarks over the noise were as follows.[15]

Good evening. This is my third visit to Duke, where it has been my experience that students are generally civil and faculty generally hostile. I am going to apologize in advance for the harsh words I will say about Duke tonight. Like every major research university, Duke is not one school but several. There are many wonderful faculties at Duke where students are trained for careers in medicine, engineering, business, and other professions. My words tonight are solely directed at the sorry state of affairs in Duke's liberal arts school, Trinity College, for reasons that will become abundantly clear.

Many departments and programs at Trinity were not happy about the prospect of my appearance here tonight and rejected the requests of the students who arranged this evening to co-sponsor the event.[16] In fact, only one academic department, Political Science, thought it might be a good idea to have an intellectual dialogue at Duke by extending a rare invitation to a conservative like myself to appear at this institution of higher learning.[17]

Things would be quite different, of course, if I were a convicted terrorist, like Laura Whitehorn, a former member of the Weather Underground who was invited to speak here in 2002 by the African and African American Studies Department. The professors who invited Whitehorn attempted to present her to unsuspecting students as a "human rights activist," until conservative students placed a paid ad in the *Duke Chronicle* informing the Duke community of her criminal record.

Or, I would be welcomed by several liberal arts faculties at Duke if I were a Jew-hating Palestinian terrorist like Professor Sami al-Arian—the North American head of Palestinian Islamic Jihad, an organization responsible for over a hundred suicide bombings of innocent civilians in the Middle East. If this were my credential, I would have been invited by a collection of Duke departments, who put together a symposium on "National Security and Civil Liberties" and invited Professor al-Arian to be the keynote speaker for their event, speaking as a civil libertarian of course. This travesty also took place in 2002. Too bad Professor al-Arian can't come back this year, because he's in jail.[18]

Or if, like Professor Norman Finkelstein, I were a self-declared enemy of Israel whose main claim to fame was writing a book describing the Holocaust as an industry which money-grubbing Jews exploit to enrich themselves further, I would also be welcomed by Duke's academic departments, as he was recently.

Or perhaps if, like Harry Belafonte, I were a washed-up calypso singer who thought the Bush administration was the Third Reich and had called Colin Powell a "house slave," I might be invited to keynote Martin Luther King Day, a $45,000 event held just weeks ago. The president of the university would then be in attendance and the provost would describe me as an Old Testament prophet, and sixteen hundred Duke students would be assembled to witness the spectacle.

The annual Martin Luther King Day celebration at Duke, whose planning is in the hands of the campus left, has invited a parade of radical speakers to keynote the event since I first began paying attention some years ago. It has featured Angela Davis, a lifelong Communist and devoted servant of totalitarian police states, and Aaron Magruder, a racially divisive cartoonist who has attacked Condoleezza Rice, the most accomplished African American woman in our history, in the most vulgar and contemptible terms. In his King Day speech, which followed closely on the heels of 9/11, Magruder honored Dr. King by noting that only

10 percent of Americans opposed their country's response to the atrocity that had been inflicted on them, and hoped that all those so alienated from their own country were black.

Yet another King Day speaker, law professor Lani Guinier, is distinguished by her advocacy of voting quotas for minorities because she doesn't trust white people not to be racist.

I wonder if it has occurred to anyone that the theme common to every one of these speakers is the denigration of the legacy of the man to be honored. Martin Luther King was the author of the most rapid and peaceful revolution in social relations in the history of nations. On the other hand, the common theme of speakers at Duke University's Martin Luther King Day ceremonies is that nothing has really changed in the condition of black people in America since the days of segregation and slavery. To hear them tell it, America is still a racist society just the way it was before King launched his campaign. Indeed, since America is the Third Reich, and blacks are obviously America's Jews, it is arguably worse.

In short, the meaning of Martin Luther King Day as celebrated at Duke is the denial of what King actually stood for, in particular his faith in the American dream as well as everything he accomplished in his efforts to realize that dream. For the leftists who orchestrate these "remembrances," the purpose of King Day is, in fact, to exploit King's name in the service of their own political agendas—radical, racially divisive, and contemptuous of the country he loved.

Another disturbing aspect of Duke's King Day festivities is their not so subtle racial subtext. Why are all the featured speakers black at an event whose purpose is to celebrate a man whose dream was a colorblind society? Why aren't Jews invited to keynote the King Day program? Does anyone believe the civil rights movement would have succeeded without the support of white Americans in general and Jews in particular? More than 50 percent of the freedom riders who volunteered to go to the South and risk their lives to support their black sisters and brothers were Jews.

A Jew created the NAACP Legal Defense Fund and was the legal strategist behind the court actions that ended segregation. A Jew was Martin Luther King's chief strategist and fund-raiser. Yet Jews are not a featured part of Duke's Martin Luther King Day celebrations and there are probably no departments more hostile to Jews on this campus than the departments that control the King Day agenda, most particularly the same African and African American Studies Department that invited a terrorist to speak.

I have in my hand here a book—to borrow a famous phrase you will no doubt recognize. It obviously *is* a book and not a "list" as its enemies have claimed. Its title is *The Professors: The 101 Most Dangerous Academics,* and it is 112,000 words and 450 pages long. The text includes a 15,000-word argument about the nature of the university and its present condition. It is based on twenty years of visits to campuses like Duke, during which I interviewed thousands of students, talked to many professors and administrators, and reflected at length on these issues.

So why do you suppose the left promotes the idea that this is a list, when it is not a list, and when the only lists of "dangerous professors" are those compiled by left-wing websites in order to attack the book? "Lists," "witch-hunts," "McCarthyite," along with other terms like "racist," "sexist," "homophobe," and "reactionary," are political weapons the left deploys to stigmatize and discredit and ultimately silence people who get in its way. If you trip on the wrong word or laugh at the wrong joke, you are a *racist.* If you let a remark slip that is politically incorrect—say, that women might have different mathematical aptitudes than men—you can be accused of *sexism* and of plotting to undermine the self-esteem of little girls. If you are the president of Harvard, such a speculation can get you censured and terminate your career.

Many people object to the subtitle of my book—*The 101 Most Dangerous Academics.* What they seem to be asking is, "How can a professor, *my* professor, be dangerous?" For someone to suggest that professors who openly call for America to be defeated in the war on terror might actually be dangerous is seen as an incitement to *persecute* them. It is *McCarthyism*. In other words, it is an unthinkable thought, which needs to be suppressed.

Individuals who react this way obviously don't think that ideas have consequences. Such people are inclined to forget (or deny) that we are actually in a war with religious fanatics who want to kill every one of us because we are infidels and reject their faith. Here is the front page of today's *Raleigh-Durham News and Observer.* As you can see, the lead story is about a Muslim student at the University of North Carolina in Chapel Hill, not far from this school, who rented a Jeep, drove it onto campus and ran it into a crowd of students with intent to kill, and sent six of them to the hospital.[19]

An idea inspired this man to try to murder innocent strangers who attended school with him. His idea was to serve Allah by murdering infidels in the country he holds responsible for Muslim deaths on the other side of the globe. His idea is that America is the Great Satan. This is an idea not really dissimilar from ideas heard in classrooms on this campus and on Martin Luther King Day—that America is the greatest terrorist state and a global "Third Reich." If you believe that and trumpet it far and wide enough, there are bound to be some people who will try to act on it.

There are an impressive number of courses and events on this campus whose clear purpose is to persuade students that America is a racist, sexist, and oppressive empire that deserves to be attacked. Just weeks ago, the Martin Luther King Day speaker told sixteen hundred students and the president of this university that he couldn't tell the difference between the terrorist Mohammed Atta and America's elected president, George Bush. If one believes that, one will also believe that Americans deserve to be attacked. Ideas have consequences.

The Professors is an argument about the intellectual corruption of America's universities. It could hardly be better illustrated than by the invitation to an extreme America-hater like Harry

Belafonte to keynote an event honoring Martin Luther King. Large parts of Duke and similar institutions across the country have been transformed into indoctrination programs in radical agendas. Entire academic departments have been transformed into what are in effect political parties. The Women's Studies Department at Duke, as at many other campuses, is not an academic enterprise devoted to scholarship about women. It is the party of feminism. It is the party of a radical feminism that sees America as a capitalist patriarchy—oppressive and imperial—and the root cause of the attacks upon it.

There are other programs at Duke that are equally nonacademic and equally radical. The "Perspectives on Marxism and Society Program" is described in the Duke catalog as a course in the theories of Marxism. Marxism is a complex subject for study. Since 1917, Marxist theories have been directly responsible for the murder of tens of millions of people. In China alone, an estimated fifty million people starved to death because China's revolutionaries tried to apply the crackpot economic theories of Marx to agricultural production.

But the Marxism and Society Program at Duke is not a program offered by the Economics or Sociology or History Department, where these failures could be analyzed by qualified experts in the field. It is offered by the *Literature* Department, and thus taught by individuals who lack professional expertise in economics, sociology, political science and history, the very fields required to evaluate a theory like Marxism. The director of the Marxism and Society Program at Duke is a professor of literature named Jane Gaines. In fact, Professor Gaines is not even a professor of literature in any meaningful sense. She is a film critic—literature having been dumbed down in institutions like Duke to include popular (and nonliterary) arts like film. Professor Gaines' entire academic output consists of writings about the movies.

How can someone whose expertise is cinema be academically qualified to direct courses in a theory that purports to explain the most complex economic, social and political developments of human societies? How can literary scholars evaluate a theory that led to the creation of the most oppressive political regimes in human history? The Marxism and Society Program is not an academic program seeking to conduct a dispassionate examination of Marxism and its consequences. It was not conceived to make a dispassionate academic appraisal of this theory and its influences. It was created by Michael Hardt, a Duke professor of comparative literature who has made his mark attempting—without training in economics or any other relevant field—to *resurrect* Marxism as a theory of the contemporary world. He is, in other words, an ideologue and amateur whose work is made possible by an academic institution that has no regard for academic standards.

According to his official Duke website, "Michael Hardt's recent writings deal primarily with the legal, economic and social aspects of globalization. In his books with Antonio Negri he has analyzed the functioning of the current global power structure (*Empire,* 2001)." But Hardt is professor of comparative literature. His professional training is language and works of fiction. Professionally speaking, Hardt is an academic imposter and his most famous "scholarly" work, *Empire,* is the work of an academic dilettante. These facts don't prevent the current academic administration at Duke from boasting of his achievements as though they were actually scholarly or expert. Hardt's co-author Antonio Negri, by the way, is a Communist who was tried, convicted and sentenced to thirty years in prison by an Italian court for promoting terrorism in his native land.

These are the intellectual origins and bona fides of the Marxism and Society curriculum at Duke, a university ranked fifth in the nation in quality by *U.S. News and World Report.*

Ideas have consequences. At universities like Duke, American students are being taught to despise their own country, and are barraged with paranoid delusions about America as an oppressive empire and a society pervaded by "institutional racism." How do these claims square with the American reality? If America is a racist country that oppresses black people, why do Haitians want to come here? Why would "people of color" from all over the world struggle so hard to become immigrants? These are the indisputable facts. Millions of "minorities" want to come here, but none of them want to leave. The obvious reason is that they are freer in this country, more privileged, and with more opportunities and rights as Americans than they enjoy in the countries of their origin, where they are a majority. That's the reality. But inside the university it is outmoded and fraudulent ideas like Marxism and its derivatives that are the reality; inside the university, intellectual reactionaries teach the myth that America is an oppressor nation, the Third Reich incarnate.

Our democracy is engaged in a war on terror. It is important to appreciate one's country when it is under attack, particularly when it is under attack from religious fanatics who may soon have access to weapons of mass destruction, and who will have no compunction about using them. The left likes to say that America is a society founded on slavery, and that this fact tainted its founding. It is true that America inherited a slave system, but that is an unremarkable truth in the context of the human record. Slavery has existed in every human society. Everyone in this audience, if one were to go far back enough, is descended from slaves, regardless of race.

What is remarkable about America is not that it inherited a slave system but that this nation was founded on the idea that slavery was wrong, that everyone is endowed by their Creator with inalienable rights to liberty and life. This revolutionary idea, which is America's birthright, led to the end of slavery in less than two generations, and not just in the United States but throughout the Western Hemisphere and in most of the world. It is an idea that still inspires the struggle for freedom across the globe. *This* is what is remarkable about America: it is a light among the nations in the struggle for freedom.

What is remarkable about America is not where we started from but where we have come to. The war in Iraq, whatever else you may think about it, is a war for freedom. Even if America is ultimately defeated in its mission in Iraq, we have made an effort to bring freedom to the Iraqi people, and to the Muslim peoples of the Middle East. This is an effort to be proud of. It is disgraceful that with few exceptions—Christopher Hitchens and Paul Berman are two that are notable—the political left has turned its back on this struggle.

In the war in Iraq, one can see the face of America: The general in charge of Central Command during the campaign to overthrow Saddam Hussein was John Abizaid, an Arab American. The general in charge of our troops inside Iraq during the overthrow of the Saddam tyranny was Ricardo Sanchez, a Hispanic American. The chief presidential adviser on the war in Iraq, first as head of the National Security Council, now as secretary of state representing America to the entire world, is an African American woman who grew up in Birmingham, in the segregated South, and saw her childhood friend blown up by racists. Condoleezza Rice is now the most powerful woman in the world. It is not where America started that is remarkable, but where we have come to.

There has never, in the history of the world, been a country like America. Unlike the mythical oppressor whose "history" is presented to students at Duke, this is a country to be proud of. And it is important to be proud of your country, in an hour when it is at war: Because if you are not proud of your country, you cannot defend yourself.

After I left Duke, I wrote a letter to the president of the university, Richard Broadhead, about the disruption led by Professor Nelson, which was an attack on academic values and a violation of Duke's own rules of conduct. "As you know," I said, "Duke has clear and unambiguous policies which forbid the obstruction of invited speakers and which require faculty to behave in a manner that reflects well on Duke as an educational institution. The behavior of Professor Nelson and her faculty colleagues was more than unprofessional and a violation of university rules. It was disrespectful of the students who had worked so hard to put this event together, of the students who came to listen and to learn, and of Duke as an institution of higher learning." I concluded by expressing the hope that he would do something to remedy the situation, which in my mind would be expressing institutional disapproval for the outrageous conduct of one his professors.

My letter to President Broadhead went unanswered. Like Dean Steinberger of Reed University, Professor Nelson was an officer of her university. Both broke a university code or, in Professor Nelson's case, an explicit university regulation. But where the president and the academic community of Reed acted to defend university standards, Duke's did not.

SIX

Battle Lines

In all conflicts, a determined adversary has the ability to determine the battleground. The controversy over academic freedom is no exception. By relying heavily on misrepresentation and personal assaults, opponents of the academic freedom campaign have left little room for negotiation or compromise. (Perhaps this is their objective.)

Prominent among these opponents is William Scheuerman, a political science professor who is the head of the SUNY professors' union and vice president of the American Federation of Teachers.[1] One of Scheuerman's typically ham-fisted attacks was the editorial in the AFT paper that was titled "Academic Bull of Rights." This broadside was also printed as a leaflet and distributed by members of his union at my campus appearances. According to Scheuerman, "The Academic Bill of Rights is nothing more than a quota system for political extremists so they can deliver their right-wing political sermons in the classroom." And further: "In case you think this version of McCarthyism has no place in the United States, think again. Several state legislatures are actually considering a bill to implement it."[2] How a bill forbidding the hiring of professors for their political views could be characterized as a "quota system for political extremists" or a "version of McCarthyism," Scheuerman didn't explain, and apparently didn't need to as far as his members were concerned.

But Scheuerman did attempt to explain—at least in his own mind—the paradox of how a campaign to take politics *out* of classrooms would nonetheless make it possible for the same classrooms to be used for "right-wing political sermons." He did this first by ignoring the clear meaning of the campaign's statements on the matter, and then by forgetting the outrage that he and his organization had expressed at the provision that professors should not introduce "controversial matter that has no relation to the subject," and finally by imputing to me, personally, an agenda I do not have:

> [Horowitz's] goal of intellectual diversity directly contradicts the principle of ideological neutrality in the classroom, the bedrock of his Academic Bill of Rights. If professors should keep their politics out of the classroom, as Horowitz argues, why should a dearth of conservatives in the classroom matter? It only matters if they plan to use the classroom as a platform for preaching a conservative ideology, which is precisely what they want to do.[3]

Is it really necessary to explain to a professor of political science that conservatism—like liberalism—is a philosophical worldview and not just a political practice? That a conservative point of view in the classroom does not mean a conservative *political* agenda in the classroom? No one is attempting to prevent teachers from expressing their *professional* views—which are commonly liberal—in the classroom. Scheuerman's assertion that a campaign to take politics out of the classroom is really a plot to make the classroom "a platform for preaching a conservative ideology" makes no sense, except as an expression of his own desperation to find an argument against the Academic Bill of Rights, and to attack it by any means available.

Scheuerman's editorial was also distributed at the annual convention of the American Federation of Teachers, which was held in Minneapolis in April 2005. According to a reporter attending the event, convention participants were preoccupied with the academic freedom campaign:

Horowitz, the creator of the Academic Bill of Rights, was on everyone's mind at the meeting, with AFT leaders vowing an all-out campaign against the legislation in both its federal and state versions. . . .
William E. Scheuerman, chair of the AFT's higher education division, called the legislation "crazy," "Orwellian," and McCarthyite.
Scheuerman, president of United University Professions, which represents faculty members at the State University of New York, said
that the legislation's provisions requiring equal representation of
views on controversial issues would require courses on the Holocaust to change so that "on Monday we would hear that the Holocaust was bad, on Wednesday that it was good, and on Friday that
it never happened."[4]

This, again, was typical. There is no clause in the Academic
Bill of Rights or in any legislation that would require "equal representation of views on controversial issues," let alone proposals
to require courses to be structured in the way Scheuerman fan-
tasized. In speech after speech and testimony after testimony,
spokesmen for the academic freedom campaign have stressed the
fact that the Academic Bill of Rights says nothing of the kind.[5]
On the other hand—and on Scheuerman's watch—Holocaust
deniers *already* teach on the faculties of universities like DePaul
and even manage to have their anti-Semitic articles circulated by
the American Association of University Professors at international conferences. But why should Scheuerman let these realities interfere with his crusade against the Academic Bill of Rights?

In June, following the teachers' convention, the American
Council on Education—an organization that represents every
major collegiate institution in the country—took an unexpected
step in recognizing the validity of our concerns. In a "Statement
on Student Academic Rights and Responsibilities," the council
addressed the problems we had highlighted and supported reme-
dies along the lines we had proposed. Its statement began: "Intellectual pluralism and academic freedom are central principles of
American higher education," which was exactly what we had
maintained. Although the council did not mention our campaign
by name, our efforts were noted: "Recently, these issues have

captured the attention of the media, political leaders and those in the academy. This is not the first time in the nation's history that these issues have become public controversies, but the current interest in intellectual discourse on campus suggests that the meaning of these terms, and the rights and responsibilities of individual members of the campus community, should be reiterated."[6] The statement also declared that there should be no political harassment of students and professors and that grievance machinery should be created at every school to resolve problems.

I publicly welcomed the American Council on Education statement as a victory for our campaign and met with Terry Hartle, one of its executive officers. Hartle told me that his staff had been pressured by university presidents to make such a statement because they felt the need for a "defensible position" in the face of our criticism. On the other hand, even before noting that the American Association of University Professors had joined the signers, I was aware that the statement might be only a boilerplate and that however useful this endorsement was, it probably did not represent a substantive change.

The real problem remained that of seeing that the principles were put into effect. A year later, these concerns were confirmed by a report issued by the American Council of Trustees and Alumni, an organization whose leader Anne Neal had testified in Pennsylvania and was a partner in our campaign. The report showed that not a single university had taken steps to implement the provisions of the statement by the American Council on Education.[7]

Nonetheless, Scheuerman was appalled by the council's position and by the fact that the American Association of University Professors had signed it: "I find it astounding that the AAUP endorsed the statement," Scheuerman told *InsideHigherEd.com.* "Some faculty leaders," the reporter commented, "said that the association shouldn't have been involved with efforts to satisfy David Horowitz."[8]

Despite all the indications that Scheuerman would use any means to thwart our efforts, I made a decision to approach him and see if he was willing to move towards a more constructive path of engagement. Quixotic as this might seem, I thought there was cause for optimism in a statement he had made in testimony at the Temple University hearings on academic freedom, when he told the legislators, "As professors we teach; we don't preach."

Instead of regarding this statement as another smokescreen for bad intentions, I seized on it as an opportunity to take Scheuerman at his word. Before he was able to leave the hearing room, I engaged him in conversation. His response to my overture was disarmingly civil, and he was evidently amused at the fact that I would even think of approaching him after all his negative comments about me.

I began our conversation by explaining to him that I had no desire to remove left-wing professors from faculties and in fact had publicly defended the notorious Ward Churchill when the governor of Colorado demanded that he be fired from his position at the University of Colorado in Boulder. In a *Rocky Mountain News* column, I pointed out the obvious fact that the First Amendment protected Churchill's free speech, however reprehensible it might be. I had never called for the firing of anyone for their political views, and—as I have had to reiterate on many occasions—the first principle of my Academic Bill of Rights forbids such censorship. I also assured Scheuerman that it was not my intention nor any part of the design of the Academic Bill of Rights to force professors to provide equal time for all points of view, least of all for crackpot views, like those of Holocaust deniers—or Ward Churchill, for that matter.

After laying down these cards, I suggested that Scheuerman invite me to one of his union events where I could meet with his colleagues to discuss their concerns about the Academic Bill of Rights in a civil and constructive manner. Perhaps we could find grounds for a compromise that might allay their concerns and lead to a revision of the document and resolution of the controversy that was by now so bitter it was destructive to his interests as well as mine. When I finished, the silence was long, and I realized my proposal was not going to be accepted. Finally, Scheuerman said, "Why don't you invite *me* to one of *your* events?"

Without hesitation, I said I would. In April, then only two months away, I was planning to hold an Academic Freedom Conference in Washington, D.C., and would put him on a panel where he could present his case. I also invited Terry Hartle of the American Council on Education to be on the panel and asked another critic of mine, Scott Jaschik, editor of *InsideHigherEd.com,* to moderate the session. In addition, I waived any admission charge to accommodate three tables of union officials from the AAUP and the NEA as well as Scheuerman's AFT. This group included his lieutenant, Jamie Horwitz, who, in addition to being a union executive, served as the press contact for the Free Exchange coalition—the group that had been created to attack *The Professors.*

The Academic Freedom Conference took place on April 7, 2006, at the Washington Court Hotel. Over the speakers' dais a twelve-foot banner stated the theme of our campaign so prominently no one could miss it: "TAKE POLITICS OUT OF THE CLASSROOM!" In my remarks I pointed to the banner and looked directly at the union officials present and said, "It doesn't say take left-wing politics out of the classroom, and let right-wing politics in. It says 'Take Politics Out of the Classroom,' period. Take all politics—left or right—out of the classroom."[9]

Before Scheuerman's session, we scheduled a panel of seven students whose presentations provided him with all the evidence he needed that preaching—not teaching—was taking place in many college classrooms, and that nothing was being done about it. In short, the Academic Bill of Rights was not "a solution in search of a problem,"[10] as he had claimed.

One of the student speakers, Mason Harrison, who was attending the University of California, Davis, described how he had enrolled in a Women's Studies class after being offered a $50 bet by his girlfriend that he wouldn't be able to handle the politically charged curriculum. Mason lost the bet on the first day of class when the professor, a political opponent of California's future governor, Arnold Schwarzenegger, led the students on a chant of "No on Arnold, no on recall!" He then enrolled in a class on counterterrorism in which the professor told students that the "number one Middle Eastern terrorist" was Jesus Christ. Next, Temple student Marlene Kowal spoke. She had enrolled in a course on "Contemporary China" in which the professor told the class that "Communism has been given a bad name in this country," and that "the only reason why Mao Zedong is given the bad reputation he has is because of the bourgeois press and their racism toward the Chinese. . . . I am a Maoist and my intention in teaching this class is to demonstrate to you why Mao was a great figure."[11]

Following these testimonies, the Scheuerman panel debated whether the legislation for an Academic Bill of Rights was necessary or advisable.[12] SUNY trustee Candace de Russy and Colorado regent Tom Lucero also participated in the discussion, which was intellectual and civil. At the end of the panel, when Scheuerman left for another engagement, we exchanged friendly goodbyes, and he thanked me for inviting him. In that moment, I actually was led to believe the encounter might have accomplished something.

But a week later, an editorial appeared in his union paper that dispelled any illusions I might have had. It was written by Scheuerman and was titled "Have You No Sense of Decency, Sir?" This was the famous put-down that attorney Joseph Welch had delivered to Senator McCarthy, after McCarthy accused a young lawyer on Welch's staff of having Communist associations. In big red letters at the top of Scheuerman's editorial were these words: "Arthur Miller wrote *The Crucible* about the Salem Witch Trials and the witch-hunts of the 1950s. The message of the play was that every period of history needs to be vigilant about similar cases of hysteria. The 'Academic Bill of Rights' is our witch-hunt."[13]

To be sure, Scheuerman wrote the article prior to our conference. But it was also after the overture I had made to him at
Temple and the reassurances I had given him as to my purposes.
These gestures and my invitation had not even produced a pause
in his attacks. In May, I spoke to students on the Cortland campus of the State University of New York. One of Scheuerman's
union professors showed up at the event to distribute a reprint
of his original "Bull of Rights" editorial denouncing my efforts
as "McCarthyism."

In the course of the academic freedom campaign, I had become
increasingly aware that the problem of political indoctrination in
the classroom was not confined to collegiate institutions, but had
spread to the primary and secondary schools as well. This was a
logical consequence of its origins in a political movement that
had targeted the educational system as a Gramscian platform to
advance its agenda, along with the fact that K-12 teachers were
trained and credentialed in the education schools of the universities themselves.

At the Academic Freedom Conference, time was set aside
to present an award to a sixteen-year-old high school student
named Sean Allen. He had become nationally famous two months
before, when he recorded the classroom remarks of his geography teacher, Jay Bennish, whose comments were more accurately
described as a tirade, shouted at his students. In a twenty-minute
rant, Bennish compared the president of the United States to
Adolf Hitler and claimed that the victims of 9/11 were not "innocent people" but "military targets," because they worked for companies "that are directly involved in the military-industrial complex
in supporting corrupt dictatorships in the Middle East. And so
in the minds of al-Qaeda, they're not attacking innocent people
... [but] people who have blood on their hands as far as they're
concerned."[14]

And that was not all. "Make sure you get these definitions down," said Bennish. "Capitalism: If you don't understand the economic system of capitalism, you don't understand the world in which we live. OK. Economic system in which all or most of the means of production, etcetera, are owned privately and operated in a somewhat competitive environment for the purpose of producing PROFIT! Of course, you can shorten these definitions down. Make sure you get the gist of it. Do you see how when, you know, when you're looking at this definition, where does it say anything about capitalism is an economic system that will provide everyone in the world with the basic needs that they need? Is that a part of this system? Do you see how this economic system is at odds with humanity? At odds with caring and compassion? It's at odds with human rights. Anytime you have a system that is designed to procure profit, when profit is the bottom motive—money—that means money is going to become more important potentially than what? Safety, human lives, etcetera."

This was a clear case of using an educational setting for political propaganda. Allen's tape was played by radio and TV talkshow hosts across the country, producing a public outcry, and Bennish was suspended for two weeks with pay while the local school authorities decided on a response. Their decision was to reinstate Bennish while warning him against further outbursts. No policy changes were made. Sean Allen, on the other hand, was faced with such hostility from teachers and students that he had to leave the school and enroll in another institution.

Bennish's outburst took place in a geography class, which might explain the economic illiteracy of his remarks. But the episode itself was by no means the expression of one eccentric's misreading of what the profession of teaching at the K-12 level should be about. Bennish's "lecture" was in fact the reflection of a well-established movement among professional educators to transform K-12 classrooms into platforms for radical politics. It refers to itself as the "social justice movement" in K-12 education.[15]

Eric Gutstein, one of the leaders of this movement, is an associate professor of mathematics education at the University of Illinois. For seven years he taught mathematics to seventh-graders at a Chicago public school. On the first anniversary of 9/11, the City of Chicago and its public schools observed three minutes of silence in memory of the victims of the Islamic attack. When it was over, Gutstein's seventh-graders began to ask questions and he let them continue to do so for "about fifteen minutes." Then he asked them what they supposed people in other countries thought about 9/11: "I put on the overhead a photo of a rally held in Islamabad, Pakistan, on September 15, 2001. The photo showed several men holding a large banner that said, 'Think! Why You Are Hated All Over the World?' "

The banner was held and guarded by men in Muslim garb, but Gutstein didn't ask the students what this might signify—for example, that the demonstration might have been staged by Muslim militants. Instead, when one of the students mentioned America's military intervention in Afghanistan, he told the class that "none of the hijackers were thought to be Afghan." Gutstein did not tell them that the government of Afghanistan had provided a base for the attackers. Instead, "I . . . shared some history, available to anyone who digs, reads, and remembers, but not widely propagated in mainstream media—the CIA involvement in Afghanistan and its funding of the *Taliban* and the *mujahideen* (anti-Soviet resistance) in the amount of well over $4 billion."[16] After about "40 minutes," Gutstein writes, "we returned to doing mathematics." But one of the students wanted to know if he "would fight against Iraq or Afghanistan. I told him that I would not because I did not believe in going to war for oil, power and control."

Gutstein's account of his class is recorded in a guide he has written for teachers—*Reading and Writing the World with Mathematics: Toward a Pedagogy for Social Justice.* It is a book on how to use K-12 mathematics classrooms for what Gutstein calls "partisan teaching"—which, as he describes it, is teaching seventh-grade children radical politics.[17] Gutstein's book is part of a series of similar books described by the publisher as "Critical Social Thought," which includes titles like *Capitalist Schools: Explanation and Ethics in Radical Studies of Schooling* and *Power and Method: Political Activism and Educational Research*. The series is edited by a University of Wisconsin professor of education and published by a prestigious academic imprint, Routledge. Gutstein's book in this series is dedicated to a shadowy group ("whom I cannot name") whom the author thanks "for allowing me to share the struggles for a better collective future for us all."[18]

The Academic Freedom Conference we held in Washington was also an event designed to launch an academic freedom campaign for K-12 schools. Today the gravest threat to American public education comes from education professionals, like Gutstein, who are determined to use primary and secondary school classrooms to indoctrinate students in radical ideology and to recruit them for radical political agendas. This indoctrination takes place under the rubric of "social justice" education, which is a left-wing shorthand for opposition to America's traditions of individual justice and free-market economics.

Proponents of social justice teaching argue that American society is inherently "oppressive" and "systemically" racist, "sexist" and "classist," and thus discriminates institutionally against women, nonwhites, working Americans and the poor. As citizens, they have a right to do so. But as educators, they do not have a right to propagandize these views in the classroom or to make them the central focus of their educational programs for students in America's public schools.

Social justice teaching violates the professional obligations of teachers in a democracy to educate students and not indoctrinate them. Such indoctrination not only violates the professional obligations of educators, it undermines America's democratic commitment to providing an academic education for all of the nation's children. Social justice education, however, is not a marginal feature of the schools of education that train the nation's teachers.

Social justice educators enjoy the full support of professional education organizations and schools across the country. The National Council for Accreditation of Teacher Education, the largest accrediting agency of teacher education programs in the United States, says that if an education school "has described its vision for teacher preparation as 'Teachers as Agents of Change' and has indicated that a commitment to social justice is one disposition it expects of teachers who can become agents of change, then it is expected that unit assessments include some measure of a candidate's commitment to social justice."

The effects of these policies are manifest in the overtly political nature of many of the nation's 1,500 education schools—the institutions responsible for training the next generation of K-12 teachers. For example, Brooklyn College's School of Education bases its evaluations of aspiring teachers in part on their commitment to "social justice." The college recently released a statement saying, "Our teacher candidates and other school personnel are prepared to demonstrate a knowledge of, language for, and the ability to create educational environments based on various theories of social justice." Humboldt State University in northern California requires prospective high school history and social studies teachers to take a course in "Social Studies Methods," whose professor, Gayle Olsen-Raymer, explains in her syllabus: "It is not an option for history teachers to teach social justice and social responsibility; it is a mandate."

The education schools are in fact among the most extreme examples of the intrusion of radical agendas into the academic curriculum, and social justice educators have organized a powerful movement to shape the teacher training programs in universities. Among its leaders is Professor William Ayers, a former head of the terrorist Weather Underground and self-proclaimed "street fighting communist," whose expressed regret on September 11, 2001, was that he and his fellow terrorists "didn't bomb enough."[19] Implausible as it may seem, Ayers is currently the Distinguished Professor of Education and Senior University Scholar at the University of Illinois at Chicago. Ayers is also the inspirer and editor of a twelve-volume Columbia Teachers College series, "Teaching for Social Justice."

Among these teacher guides are titles like *Teaching Social Justice for Science* and *Teaching Social Justice for Mathematics.* Peter McClaren, professor of education at UCLA, an influential theorist of the "teaching for social justice" movement, is the author of a widely read book describing Che Guevara, who directed mass political executions in Cuba, as the most important pedagogue of the twentieth century. The outgoing and incoming presidents of the 25,000-member American Education Research Association, the major umbrella organization of the education school professorate, are both supporters of the doctrine of teaching for social justice in K-12 classrooms. The Education Research Association has just hired its first "director of social justice."

Programmatic radicalism is not incidental to social justice education but lies at its core. Lee Anne Bell, director of the Education Program at Columbia's Barnard College, is co-editor of the book *Teaching for Diversity and Social Justice,* a text for prospective K-12 teachers, in which she explains that social justice education is necessary because American society "is steeped in oppression." Most oppressive of all, Bell contends, is free-market capitalism, which she defines as an "economic system that structures and requires" poverty. The chapter on "Designing Social Justice Education Courses" in Professor Bell's text states that "Courses can have a single issue focus (racism or classism for example) or a multiple issue focus (sexism, heterosexism, and ableism [a term to describe discrimination against people with disabilities])."

Even a subject seemingly removed from the realm of politics—mathematics—is a vehicle for political indoctrination in the hands of social justice educators. The Master of Education program at Northeastern University offers a course to K-12 teachers called "Teaching Mathematics for Social Justice." *Rethinking Mathematics: Teaching Social Justice by the Number* is one prominent text in this field. Its editors, Eric Gutstein and Bob Peters, are both public school math teachers and their textbook is intended to "provide examples of how to weave social justice throughout the mathematics curriculum." The authors include "teaching suggestions" in the book, among which are an exercise to calculate the cost of the Iraq war; a "math project about racial profiling"; a lesson on reading line graphs detailing "corporate control of U.S. media"; and even a cartography lesson where students consider a "map of territory that the United States took from Mexico."

Since its inception, public education in America has been about creating the next generation of citizens of a democracy, meaning individuals who can think for themselves, not citizens who are force-fed orthodoxies or doctrines of a sectarian nature. The mission of America's elementary and secondary schools has traditionally been to serve American pluralism: to educate a community of citizens who disagree with each other into a common culture of tolerance and respect. The goal of America's public schools is encapsulated on the Seal of the United States: *E Pluribus Unum,* "Out of Many, One."

The leftist political agenda of social justice educators undermines this traditional vision of the role of the American public school system. The historical ideal of public schooling as a means of assimilating all children, and particularly the children of recent immigrants, into a common civic and democratic culture is now under assault by education professors advocating social justice and class conflict and deriding the ideal of a common civic culture as nothing more than capitalist hegemony. A democracy cannot tolerate the corruption of its educational system by a political faction, whatever its persuasion. A diverse community like America's cannot be sustained if its taxpayer-supported educational system becomes the captive of one political faction, particularly one whose agenda is the destruction of that community.

Just before Memorial Day, 2005, I had a chance to view an attempt by radical public school teachers to propagandize their students close up. Through circumstances that I will briefly relate, I managed to invite myself to what turned out be a propaganda offensive against America's military presence in Iraq, at a high school in the Pacific Palisades, a suburb of Los Angeles. The in-school event was a production of the school's English Department, which had corralled three hundred students for a lecture of an hour and forty-five minutes, during school hours, to be delivered by a former CIA analyst and antiwar activist. The speaker had been provided by an organization called "U.S. Tour of Duty," a group that works to actively obstruct America's war against terror.[20] The outside organizer of the event was a former member of the Palisades High School English Department named Marcy Winograd, who is president of Progressive Democrats, representing the extreme left of the Democratic Party, and a member of Palisadians for Peace, an organization of left-wing activists opposed to the war.

My appearance at the event was unplanned and the result of a series of unlikely circumstances. I had been contacted a week prior to the event by Jeff Norman, the organizer for U.S. Tour of Duty, asking if I would debate a former CIA analyst named Ray McGovern, who was now part of the Cindy Sheehan movement against the American military. The proposed venue for our debate—a church in Venice, California—did not appeal to me, since the area was gang-infested and I knew the audience would be composed of left-wing activists who have behaved badly and even violently at events where I have appeared in the past. I told Norman that I would not appear unless he found a more hospitable venue on the Westside or in the San Fernando Valley.

McGovern, who resided in Virginia, was in California to visit his son, so there was little flexibility in his schedule. Only one or two dates were possible and Norman indicated to me that he was having trouble securing a new venue on such short notice. At this juncture I received an e-mail from Marcy Winograd, whom I did not know, which was not addressed to me but to McGovern. Whether she copied me inadvertently I do not know. Winograd's e-mail referred to a lecture by McGovern on the war in Iraq that she had set up at Palisades High.

When I learned of this plan, I was determined to see that another viewpoint would be presented at the event. I e-mailed McGovern, suggesting that we could hold our debate at Palisades High if he was amenable. McGovern agreed. I then proposed that the topic should be "How should we look at the war in Iraq?" as a neutral formulation. Before hearing back from him, I received an e-mail from Winograd saying she wanted the topic to be "The U.S. government should rapidly terminate its occupation of Iraq. Agree. Disagree. Qualify." We settled on my formulation.

When I arrived at Palisades High School, the auditorium was already filling up. Milling among the audience, I introduced myself to more than a dozen of the teenagers and asked them if they knew why they were there. Only about four of those I questioned did. All of them said they were there because their teachers had brought them. One of the students told me the same group of English teachers had shown the same audience an anti-war film a few days earlier. Evidently, propagandizing students was a full-scale program at Palisades High. I noticed that one of the teachers present was wearing a T-shirt featuring a picture of John Brown with a political slogan advocating the use of force and violence to overthrow unjust governments. When I visited the same teacher's classroom some days later, it was adorned by posters of Che Guevara and radical labor organizer Mother Jones along with a sign that said, "Iraq is Arabic for Vietnam."

Had I not intruded myself into the McGovern event, the students would have been subjected to McGovern's unchallenged views, which were soon revealed. America's intervention in Iraq was a "war for oil" because, as he explained, "we're running out of oil," and the war on terror was caused by "America's support for Israel." He told the students that a hundred thousand innocent Iraqis had been killed by America "for no reason," and that President Bush's policy in the war was really the policy of Israel's prime minister at the time, Ariel Sharon. McGovern told the students that America should leave Iraq at once, even if it meant a bloodbath, because staying would be much worse since we were only spreading terror and killing innocents by being there in the first place. The only way to fight the war on terror, he summed up, was to "deal with the grievances of those who hate us," which in his view were principally our policies in support of Israel.

I was deeply troubled by the event, which lifted the veil from an ongoing program of indoctrination in public schools. Students I spoke to afterwards volunteered that the school was "very political" and that their teachers were very left-wing. One student told me that he had been thrown out of a class by his teacher for claiming that Saddam Hussein had used chemical weapons against his own people, a fact which the teacher denied. Other students told me their teachers constantly harangued them on controversial issues. A conservative teacher told me he was afraid to speak up because of inevitable reprisals from the faculty majority. It was a mirror image of what was happening on our college campuses.

Before leaving, I confronted several of the teachers present over what I considered to be the abuse of students in their charge. Using students as a captive audience on which to inflict their political prejudices was entirely unprofessional, I said, and a violation of the students' academic freedom. Students are in school to be educated, which necessarily included hearing several views on controversial issues and being left free to form their own. None of the teachers I spoke to acknowledged the possibility that the scene was not a normal aspect of secondary school education. When I asked the English teacher with the John Brown T-shirt why she was wearing a political slogan, and whether she had considered that it might be abusive to inflict her political opinions on her students, she accused me of being insensitive to the Muslim students present, a reference to my remarks during the debate that we were at war with "radical Islam." She had no words of concern, however, for the Jewish students present whose community had been blamed for the war on terror and the death of innocents, nor for the half a dozen Hispanic and black students who raised their hands when asked if anyone present had a brother or sister in Iraq. Apparently it was fine to bring in a political radical to tell them that American soldiers were risking their lives for oil companies and the Jews, and that the reason they were in Iraq was to kill innocent Iraqis and spread terrorism.

Walking away from Pali High, I found myself alongside the event's organizer, Marcy Winograd. "Don't you think it's abusive to inflict your political agendas on school children who are here for an education?" I asked her.

"But the media are all on the other side," she said.

"Even if your claim were correct," I answered, "the media are private institutions and are players in the nation's political debate. This is a public school. Can't you appreciate the difference?"

"The media are on the other side," she repeated, as though the thought was above her mental ceiling, and I gave up.

Academic Progress

On the eve of the April 2006 Academic Freedom Conference, I took part in a debate with Colorado University professor Ward Churchill at George Washington University. The topic was "Can Politics Be Taken Out of the Classroom—and Should It Be?" My view was that it could and should; Churchill took the negative position. "I'm a professor, and I profess," he said from the podium. He was unapologetic about his radical politics and clearly proud of the fact that he injected them into his classroom in the Ethnic Studies program at Boulder, where he was still a professor.

Churchill's description of the victims of 9/11 as "little Eichmanns" had led to the scandal that brought the problem of the radicalized university to the attention of the broad American public. Outrage over his remarks had precipitated the resignation of the president of the University of Colorado and caused enormous damage to the institution itself. Two weeks after the public eruption, I was in Boulder to give a speech and had dinner with one of the regents, who told me the university had already lost more than $10 million in cancelled student applications. University officials had been working arduously for nearly a year on the task of restoring the reputation of their school.[1]

One of the steps they took was to appoint a faculty panel to review Churchill's academic record. A year later, the panel concluded unanimously that Churchill had falsified and fabricated

historical events, plagiarized research material from other scholars, and failed to attribute sources properly.[2] A majority of the
panel members also concluded that Churchill was guilty of academic misconduct so serious as to justify the termination of his
tenured position.[3] A month later, the panel met again and voted
to recommend that Churchill be fired.[4]

These assessments were based entirely on the deficits of
Churchill's "scholarly" work, not his political polemics like the article on 9/11. The panel found "repeated instances of his practice of
fabricating details or ostensible written evidence to buttress his
broader ideological arguments," and commented: "while his general claims may be correct, it is unacceptable scholarship to create
fictitious support for them."[5] In his response, Churchill explained
his attitude towards scholarship, conceding that he conflated political activism with his academic mission: "I've got this general understanding. You say, but can that general understanding be confirmed?
Well, I'm looking to confirm it. I'm also looking for information,
and I told you this at the outset, I'm looking to prove it's true."[6]
This was the attitude of a political activist, not a scholar.

The faculty committee also noted that Churchill had no
academic credentials or expertise in the areas he chose to research:
"Although many of his writings, including nearly all those discussed in this report, address historical and/or legal issues, he does
not have formal training at the graduate level in those fields. Professors writing on the topics he addresses would typically have a
Ph.D. in history or a law degree; Professor Churchill's graduate
degree is an M.A. in Communications Theory."[7]

This lack of credentials was obviously known to university
officials and Churchill's department colleagues, who had voted
to hire him, award him tenure, promote him to a full professorship and elect him chair of the Ethnic Studies Department. But
if it had not been for the public scandal attending his article on
9/11, Churchill's career as a distinguished and tenured professor,
showered with honors in his field, would have continued undis-
turbed: "The Committee notes that this investigation was only

commenced *after,* and perhaps in response to, the public attack on Professor Churchill for his controversial publications. Some of the allegations sent to the Committee related to events that apparently had been well known by scholars in the field, although perhaps not by responsible University personnel, for years before the University took any action whatsoever concerning them, and it did so only after the controversy over Professor Churchill's essays became national news."[8]

In other words, the Churchill affair indicated a corruption of academic standards that was not confined to the malfeasance of a single individual, but was systemic. The only possible conclusion is that Churchill was hired and promoted to his elevated status on the basis of his political views, not his academic scholarship, which was nonexistent. In establishing these facts, the investigative report by a panel of Churchill's academic peers validated the concerns of the academic freedom campaign. Leaders of the American Association of University Professors and the American Federation of Teachers had repeatedly claimed that there was "no evidence" of ideological corruption of the academic enterprise. The Churchill inquiry showed irrefutably that there was.

The fact that a faculty panel had written so damning a report was encouraging. Our campaign was based on two assumptions: (1) the existence of a regime of professional standards that had been systematically violated; and (2) the existence of a majority within the academic community that was committed to those standards. Except in extraordinary circumstances, such as those generated by the public outrage over the Churchill scandal, this majority was generally intimidated by the minority into accepting its abuses. The panel's report clearly showed that an outside factor, in this case public opinion, could change the institutional dynamic that had made the corruption of the intellectual enterprise possible.

The Colorado panel also provided a commentary on the kind of opposition the campaign had faced: "Professor Churchill was likewise unwilling to acknowledge any serious wrongdoing in his conversations with our Committee, though he was civil and collegial in manner. We note, however, that his habit of responding to an accusation by disparaging the accuser rather than addressing the question serves as a way to evade genuine confrontation with the charges."[9]

Disparaging the accuser rather than addressing the question. This was the defining characteristic of the left's political strategy, and an apt description of the opposition to the Academic Bill of Rights and the campaign for intellectual diversity. A constant refrain of this opposition was that there was "no evidence" of abuses and that the claims made by students about the existence of such evidence were baseless. In a book written to refute the claims of the academic freedom campaign, Professor Michael Berube said: "Most people outside academe are thoroughly unaware of how well-organized the anti-academic right is, and how successful the Horowitz machine has been in getting its version of campus controversies represented in national media— regardless of the actual realities of the events they describe."[10]

Berube is a member of the National Council of the American Association of University Professors and one of the most outspoken critics of the Academic Bill of Rights. As an example of the fallacious claims the campaign is alleged to have made, Berube cites a case involving a Kuwaiti immigrant named Ahmad al-Qloushi. According to Berube, "[Al-Qloushi] claimed that he received a failing grade on a term paper about the U.S. Constitution because it was 'pro-American.'" As Berube notes, al-Qloushi appeared on several national media outlets and "Horowitz flogged this case as well."[11] According to Berube, the al-Qloushi case died when the term paper he wrote was published on the Web because it showed that al-Qloushi deserved a failing grade. The essay, writes Berube, is "shoddy" and "terribly written" and "not a college-level essay."[12] Further, since conservatives made the treatment of al-Qloushi an issue, the episode has far greater significance: "For any teacher who has ever encountered an incompetent essay of any kind, the elevation of al-Qloushi to the status of conservative Hero is a profound testimony to the intellectual vacuity of the anti-academic right—and the intellectual bankruptcy of the right-wing media apparatus for which such tales of atrocity and oppression are now a stock in trade."[13]

There is something distasteful, to begin with, in this intemperate attack on the writing ability of a seventeen-year-old immigrant from Kuwait who had been in the United States all of three months when he was given the assignment by his junior college professor. Moreover, without comparing al-Qloushi's paper with that of other students in the "Introduction to American Government and Politics" course at Foothill Junior College, how can Berube be so certain that this was not in fact a college-level essay for students attending this school? Would Berube exhibit the same callousness towards an immigrant student from Mexico attempting to explain her dissatisfaction, say, with American immigration policy? What made Berube's comments truly outrageous (but nonetheless typical),[14] however, was that a failing grade was not actually al-Qloushi's complaint. *His paper was not even graded.*

In an article posted on my website at *Frontpagemagazine.com,* al-Qloushi explained what his actual concerns were, about which there is not a clue in Berube's text:

> Professor Woolcock didn't grade my essay. Instead he told me to come to see him in his office the following morning. I was surprised the next morning when instead of giving me a grade, Professor Woolcock verbally attacked me and my essay. He told me, "Your views are irrational." He called me naïve for believing in the greatness of this country, and told me "America is *not* God's gift to the world." Then he upped the stakes and said "You need regular psychotherapy." Apparently, if you are an Arab Muslim who loves America you must be deranged. Professor Woolcock went as far as to threaten me by stating that he would visit the Dean of International Admissions (who has the power to take away student visas) to make sure I received regular psychological treatment.[15]

In other words, Al-Qloushi's complaint was that Professor Wool-
cock took exception to his *views,* not his writing style; that the
professor made it clear he regarded disagreement with his own
negative views of America as a form of mental disorder; and that
he made an implicit threat to an immigrant student about his res-
ident status. These are pretty serious charges and hardly demonstrate the intellectual bankruptcy of those who gave al-Qloushi
support.

But why should we believe al-Qloushi? Maybe he was making everything up to serve his (alleged) right-wing views. In fact,
Frontpagemag.com had previously published another story about
the incident by another Foothill College student—a liberal student named Michael Wiesner:

> My name is Michael Wiesner and I am a former student at Foothill
> College in Los Altos Hills, California. I am writing this article in
> the wake of an incident in which a teacher at the college recom-
> mended psychological therapy to an Arab student who had praised
> the U.S. Constitution. On December 1st, a professor named Joseph
> Woolcock suggested a Kuwaiti Arab Muslim student named Ahmad
> al-Qloushi should seek therapy after the student submitted a paper
> arguing that the U.S. Constitution was a step forward for America
> and the world. The Foothill College Republicans reported Dr. Wool-
> cock's behavior to the media, and Dr. Woolcock issued a grievance
> in a further attempt to silence the student. The college is treating
> the matter as if it is an isolated incident. They are doing everything
> they can to distance themselves from the matter. But in truth, teacher
> intimidation goes to the very heart of the Foothill College bureau-
> cracy. It has become commonplace for the school to silence students
> with ideas or opinions contrary to those of their professors.

Wiesner went on:

> Foothill College is not only a place where conservative students like
> Ahmad are low-tracked by liberal teachers. It is also a place where
> conservative professors feel free to bust down liberal students like
> me. The problem goes beyond politics. Foothill College is a place
> where teachers are free to target students they dislike, out of pique,
> race, religion, or sexual orientation, with inappropriate comments

during class, intimidation, and grade manipulation. I am writing this article because it happened to me, and I have been intimidated into silence about my ordeal for three years. It is Ahmad al-Qloushi's courage in this matter that brings me to speak about my experience. Ahmad and I are speaking out as two students at the opposite ends of the political spectrum.

Wiesner added:

> I find most of David Horowitz's right-wing views to be offensive. I led an anti-war rally at Foothill College, and I voted against George W. Bush both times. That having been said, intellectual pluralism is not a political issue. We must treat intellectual pluralism as an issue of intellectual freedom. Both liberal students and conservative students ought to be free to express their ideas in the classroom.[16]

Wiesner then went on to explain his abuse at the hands of a conservative professor, a cause in which the academic freedom movement supported him. I have quoted his comments at length because they refute the case that Berube and others have made against our campaign, which is not about right-wing agendas, or defending only conservative students, or holding only liberal professors to account; it is not based on nonexistent facts or unsubstantiated student claims; and it is not an attempt to challenge the authority of professors over the curriculum. It is, as Michael Wiesner wrote, about intellectual pluralism, about respect for students who dissent, and about protecting their right to draw their own conclusions on controversial matters.

Twenty years ago, Allan Bloom wrote a notable essay on the malign cultural influences of the 1960s, which he called *The Closing of the American Mind*. In it, Bloom described how political correctness—the radical view that history is relentlessly a record of domination and oppression—stifled intellectual debate in the academy. By holding sacrosanct the alleged victims of history's oppressions, the new dispensation exempted all groups (with the exception of white males) from accountability for what they had or had not done. The effect of this injunction was to close down the Socratic interrogation of values and lives, the very idea that had previously governed the liberal arts curriculum.

Bloom emphasized the ironies resulting from this orthodoxy, how it contorted views on McCarthyism and academic freedom: "Another aspect of the [left's] mythology is that McCarthyism had an extremely negative impact on the universities. Actually the McCarthy period was the last time the university had any sense of community, defined by a common enemy. McCarthy, those like him, and those who followed them, were clearly non-academic and anti-academic, the barbarians at the gates.... Today there are many more things unthinkable and unspeakable in universities than there were then, and little disposition to protect those who have earned the ire of the radical movements."[17]

The current movement for academic freedom—the third such wave in the modern era—has already made progress in changing this state of affairs. Two milestones in this effort were passed in the spring and summer of 2006, as a direct result of the hearings on academic freedom in Pennsylvania.

The first was a decision in May by the Faculty Senate of Penn State University to include students under the school's existing academic freedom protections, which enjoined professors from using their authority to indoctrinate students, or from persuading them to adopt the professor's personal viewpoint on matters that were controversial. Under the old policy, professors were expected to follow these professional restraints, but students had no right to object if they did not. The old policy was part of the employee manual and provided no recourse for students who wished to complain.[18] To correct this lacuna, the new Faculty Senate policy stated: "Students having concerns about situations that arise within the classroom, or concerns with instructor behavior in a course that violates University standards of classroom conduct as defined in Policy HR64 'Academic Freedom,' may seek resolution according to the recommended procedures established under Policy 20-00, Resolution of Classroom Problems."[19]

The new policy was a vindication of the academic freedom campaign's central point: that students have a right to expect professional (and not political) behavior from their professors in the classroom.

Then on July 19, the trustees of Temple University announced the adoption of a new policy that would specifically protect students from political abuses in the classroom, and provide grievance machinery to handle their complaints. During the Pennsylvania hearings, Temple student Marlene Kowal, the head of the campus chapter of Students for Academic Freedom, arranged for twenty students to meet with Temple trustees. The stories they told of inappropriate political agitation and in-class harassment were troubling enough. But even more disturbing were their responses when asked why they had not gone to university authorities to complain. Every student interviewed expressed fears of reprisal from their professors if they chose to speak up. As a result, care was taken in drawing up the new policy to ensure that student complaints would be reported to the trustees themselves and that an adequate grievance machinery would be created to hear student complaints.

The Temple document was called "Student and Faculty Academic Rights and Responsibilities" and noted: "Freedom to teach and freedom to learn are inseparable facets of academic freedom."[20] It further said: "As members of the academic community, students should be encouraged to develop the capacity for critical judgment and to engage in a sustained and independent search for the truth." In pursuit of these ends, "student performance should be evaluated solely on an academic basis and by reference to the professional standards that sustain the University's pursuit and achievement of knowledge, not on opinions or conduct in matters unrelated to the academic subject."

Equally important was the provision that set up grievance machinery for students whose rights had been infringed. The policy specified that this was to be a different grievance machinery from existing university procedures that dealt with unfair grading practices. The new procedures would specifically address the student's right to learn, free from political harassment and indoctrination. The policy further stipulated that all incoming freshmen would be apprised of their right to expect professional behavior from their professors.

By establishing these rights, the Temple policy shifted institutional power, altering the dynamic of university governance. Administrators attempting to enforce academic standards would no longer be left to face faculty by themselves. Students would become factors in the process. The previously missing link had been provided. Now administrators would act as brokers enforcing a community standard that encompassed both components of the learning process. This was precisely what the campaign for academic freedom had set out to achieve.

The Temple reforms were mainly concerned with academic manners and classroom decorum. While of fundamental importance to the educational process, however, they left the larger issue of intellectual diversity on faculties untouched, and therefore did not affect the curriculum and its problems. To remedy the abuses in these areas an entirely different innovation was needed and this proved to be the second development to emerge from the Pennsylvania hearings.

Criticism of the "illiberal education" offered by colleges has been around for almost two decades now, and along with it proposals for ways to enhance the intellectual diversity of the curriculum. Stephen Balch, president of the National Association of Scholars, for instance, had long been an advocate of curricular programs that addressed the issues of free societies and featured traditional approaches to Western civilization. He had initiated and supported several such proposals at various universities. Others had been concerned about these matters, too, notably philosophy professor and well-known conservative Robert George, who had received the blessing of the Princeton administration and the generous support of donors to design the Madison Center at Princeton. By bringing conservative lecturers and speakers to campus and conducting courses with the Princeton Department of Political Science, George's program had enriched the Princeton curriculum and expanded the intellectual horizons of Princeton's academic environment.

But the Madison Center was not approved as a full-fledged academic department and did not have the ability to hire faculty or develop its own curriculum and degree program for students. Consequently, its ability to compete with other Princeton programs and to influence the Princeton curriculum had strict and well-defined limits. To establish a true marketplace of ideas it is necessary to create new departments, which grant degrees, control their own professor lines, and report directly to the university's central administration. The academic left provided the precedent when it created the politicized fields of women's studies and black studies in the 1970s, which were followed by numerous similar interdisciplinary fields. Conservatives do not—and should not—propose creating the flip side of these ideological prototypes. To advance the twin causes of academic standards and academic freedom, it is necessary for new departments to be professional and scholarly, and not governed by political agendas like those created by the academic left.

From its inception, the academic freedom movement has looked for opportunities to make the structural changes that would introduce intellectual diversity into the academy. In conjunction with its efforts to support the academic freedom hearings in Pennsylvania, it encouraged David Saxe, a professor of education at Penn State University, to submit a proposal for the creation of a new university-wide academic faculty. The new department would report directly to the provost and would be called the "Center for the Study of Free Institutions and Civic Education." In Saxe's proposal, the agenda of the new center would be to "sponsor programs of study and extra-curricula activities dealing with the nature of free institutions and civic education within the context of traditional American history. It will be especially concerned with fostering an understanding of free institutions among those students preparing for careers in teaching, and among teachers already in service. The center will also seek to play a role in public education, organizing a variety of lectures and symposia meant to reach out to broader on-campus and off-campus audiences."

In June 2006, Saxe's proposal was accepted by Penn State president Graham Spanier and provost Rodney Erickson. In July, members of the Appropriations Committee of the Pennsylvania House of Representatives, spurred by committee member Gib Armstrong, allocated $500,000 to underwrite the new center's budget.

The Center for the Study of Free Institutions and Civic Education is one of almost two dozen new faculties in various stages of development at universities around the country. All of these projects are attempts to institute traditional standards of scholarship in liberal arts fields where they are missing in action, particularly regarding the study of Western civilization. They are designed to invigorate a marketplace of ideas that has experienced a dramatic constriction during the decades of political correctness and the regime of radical discourse. The new departments are not proposed as conservative replicas of politicized fields like women's studies, cultural studies or postcolonial studies, but as counterpoints to ideological conceptions of scholarship. The agendas are academic—to study free institutions, not to praise or denigrate them. They are proposed as departments dedicated to scholarly inquiry into the moral, economic, political and cultural foundations of free societies, which are based on philosophical individualism, private property and market economics.

David Saxe's center at Penn State and the new Temple University policy to defend students' academic freedom are first steps in the effort to reverse the trends that have politicized America's institutions of higher learning, debased their professional standards and flattened their intellectual horizons. These developments have been made possible because the movement for academic freedom has captured the imagination of students on campuses across the country, as an idea whose time has come.

The early successes of these efforts have been ironically aided by the intellectual crudeness of the opposition campaign. Asked about the campaign's success, a spokesman for the American Federation of Teachers explained to a reporter that the opposition to the Academic Bill of Rights was slow to react because "we dismissed it as the rantings of an ideologue."[21] To describe the bill as a "rant" was a self-defeating tactic. Yet three years into the campaign for an Academic Bill of Rights, the opposition was still relying on ad hominem assaults on its sponsors, self-revealing distortions of their intentions and blanket denials of the problem. Such transparent claims may have been suited for rallying the faithful, but were unable to persuade anyone else. The question was why academic organizations would resort to so crude a response. Why not concede the existence of the problem and propose a more suitable remedy?

The explanation lay in the opposition's determination to defend the ground it had seized over a thirty-year march through the institutions; its political agendas *required* the abuses. It was because academic activists wanted to establish doctrinal orthodoxies in America's liberal arts colleges that they had declared war even on liberal proposals for reform. Orthodoxies such as the tenured radicals were seeking to impose had not been a prominent feature of academic institutions since the days when colleges were still denominational. From this vantage, the politicized academy of the last few decades could be seen as a secularized version of the church school, whose purpose was to train students in a religious creed. Viewed in this perspective, the stonewalling by the opponents of academic freedom is readily understood. Professional standards and intellectual diversity are threats to their calling. Academic freedom precludes doctrinal orthodoxies and programs of indoctrination. Yet this has become the core of their identity as "scholar activists." This is the contradiction that confronts the opponents of the Academic Bill of Rights, and it is one that they cannot resolve.

For the majority both in the academy and in the nation at large who are not in thrall to these radical agendas, the problem has an urgency that can no longer be denied. The educational institutions of a pluralistic democracy provide the crucial foundations of a common culture committed to the preservation of America's pluralistic values. "Intellectual pluralism and academic freedom," in the words of the American Council on Education, "are central principles of American higher education." In the liberal arts faculties of American universities—in particular those departments and fields that form the core curriculum of a civic education—these principles are no longer honored. Yet the future of this nation as a free society depends on their being so honored again.

APPENDIX I

The Academic Bill of Rights

I. The Mission of the University[1]

The central purposes of a university are the pursuit of truth, the discovery of new knowledge through scholarship and research, the study and reasoned criticism of intellectual and cultural traditions, the teaching and general development of students to help them become creative individuals and productive citizens of a pluralistic democracy, and the transmission of knowledge and learning to society at large. Free inquiry and free speech within the academic community are indispensable to the achievement of these goals. The freedom to teach and to learn depend upon the creation of appropriate conditions and opportunities on the campus as a whole as well as in the classrooms and lecture halls. These purposes reflect the values—pluralism, diversity, opportunity, critical intelligence, openness and fairness—that are the cornerstones of American society.

II. Academic Freedom

1. THE CONCEPT. Academic freedom and intellectual diversity are values indispensable to the American university. From its first formulation in the *General Report of the Committee on Academic Freedom and Tenure* of the American Association of University Professors, the concept of academic freedom has been premised on the idea that human knowledge is a never-ending pursuit of the truth, that there is no humanly accessible truth that

is not in principle open to challenge, and that no party or intellectual faction has a monopoly on wisdom.[2] Therefore, academic freedom is most likely to thrive in an environment of intellectual diversity that protects and fosters independence of thought and speech. In the words of the *General Report,* it is vital to protect "as the first condition of progress, [a] complete and unlimited freedom to *pursue* inquiry and publish its results."

Because free inquiry and its fruits are crucial to the democratic enterprise itself, academic freedom is a national value as well. In a historic 1967 decision *(Keyishian v. Board of Regents of the University of the State of New York),* the Supreme Court of the United States overturned a New York State loyalty provision for teachers with these words: "Our Nation is deeply committed to safeguarding academic freedom, [a] transcendent value to all of us and not merely to the teachers concerned." In *Sweezy v. New Hampshire* (1957), the Court observed that the "essentiality of freedom in the community of American universities [was] almost self-evident."

2. THE PRACTICE. Academic freedom consists in protecting the intellectual independence of professors, researchers and students in the pursuit of knowledge and the expression of ideas from interference by legislators or authorities within the institution itself. This means that no political, ideological or religious orthodoxy will be imposed on professors and researchers through the hiring or tenure or termination process, or through any other administrative means by the academic institution. Nor shall legislatures impose any such orthodoxy through its control of the university budget.

This protection includes students. From the first statement on academic freedom, it has been recognized that intellectual independence means the protection of students—as well as faculty—from the imposition of any orthodoxy of a political, religious or ideological nature. The 1915 *General Report* admonished faculty to avoid "taking unfair advantage of the student's immaturity by indoctrinating him with the teacher's own opinions before the student has had an opportunity fairly to examine other opinions upon the matters in question, and before he has sufficient knowledge and ripeness of judgment to be entitled to form any definitive opinion of his own." In 1967, the AAUP's *Joint Statement on Rights and Freedoms of Students* reinforced and amplified this injunction by affirming the inseparability of "the freedom to teach and freedom to learn." In the words of the report, "Students should be free to take reasoned exception to the data or views offered in any course of study and to reserve judgment about matters of opinion."

Therefore, to secure the intellectual independence of faculty and students and to protect the principle of intellectual diversity, the following principles and procedures shall be observed.

These principles fully apply only to public universities and to private universities that present themselves as bound by the canons of academic freedom. Private institutions choosing to restrict academic freedom on the basis of creed have an obligation to be as explicit as is possible about the scope and nature of these restrictions.

1. All faculty shall be hired, fired, promoted and granted tenure on the basis of their competence and appropriate knowledge in the field of their expertise and, in the humanities, the social sciences, and the arts, with a view toward fostering a plurality of methodologies and perspectives. No faculty shall be hired or fired or denied promotion or tenure on the basis of his or her political or religious beliefs.

2. No faculty member will be excluded from tenure, search and hiring committees on the basis of their political or religious beliefs.

3. Students will be graded solely on the basis of their reasoned answers and appropriate knowledge of the subjects and disciplines they study, not on the basis of their political or religious beliefs.

4. Curricula and reading lists in the humanities and social sciences should reflect the uncertainty and unsettled character of all human knowledge in these areas by providing students with dissenting sources and viewpoints where appropriate. While teachers are and should be free to pursue their own findings and perspectives in presenting their views, they should consider and make their students aware of other viewpoints. Academic disciplines should welcome a diversity of approaches to unsettled questions.

5. Exposing students to the spectrum of significant scholarly viewpoints on the subjects examined in their courses is a major responsibility of faculty. Faculty will not use their courses for the purpose of political, ideological, religious or anti-religious indoctrination.

6. Selection of speakers, allocation of funds for speakers programs and other student activities will observe the principles of academic freedom and promote intellectual pluralism.

7. An environment conducive to the civil exchange of ideas being an essential component of a free university, the obstruction of invited campus speakers, destruction of campus literature or other effort to obstruct this exchange will not be tolerated.

8. Knowledge advances when individual scholars are left free to reach their own conclusions about which methods, facts and theories have been validated by research. Academic institutions and professional societies formed to advance knowledge within an area of research, maintain the integrity of the research process, and organize the professional lives of related researchers serve as indispensable venues within which scholars circulate research findings and debate their interpretation. To perform these functions adequately, academic institutions and professional societies should maintain a posture of organizational neutrality with respect to the substantive disagreements that divide researchers on questions within, or outside, their fields of inquiry.

Academic Freedom Code for K-12 Schools

A Code of Ethics and Professional Responsibility for Educators in K-12 Public Schools

Whereas the purpose of public education in America is to produce knowledgeable and competent adults able to participate as informed citizens in the democratic process;

Whereas this purpose is best served by offering students a curriculum that is non-partisan and non-sectarian;

Whereas it has been established through testimony at legislative hearings that many teachers in K-12 classrooms are abusing taxpayer resources and abusing their ability to speak to captive audiences of students in an attempt to indoctrinate or influence children to adopt specific political and ideological positions on issues of social and political controversy;

Whereas public school teachers are public employees who have been hired for the purpose of teaching their subjects and not for the purpose of using their classrooms as a platform for political, religious, anti-religious, or ideological advocacy;

Whereas it has been established that some teacher training institutions, teacher licensing agencies, state education departments and professional teacher organizations have condoned this behavior under the guise of "teaching for social justice" and other sectarian political doctrines;

Whereas time spent on political or ideological indoctrination takes time away from instruction in the academic subjects taught by public educational institutions including the foundational subjects of mathematics, science, English, history, and civics and prevents students from receiving the best possible public education as funded by the taxpayers of this state;

Whereas parents and taxpayers have a right to expect that taxpayer resources will be spent on education, not political or ideological indoctrination;

Therefore be it resolved that this state's [board of education or other relevant regulating body] will promulgate clear regulations for appropriate professional and ethical behavior by teachers licensed to teach in this state; that these guidelines shall make it clear that teachers in taxpayer-supported schools are forbidden to use their classrooms to try to engage in political, ideological, or religious advocacy.

At a minimum, these regulations shall provide that no teacher is permitted during class time or while otherwise operating within the scope of employment as a teacher in a public educational institution to do the following (these provisions do not apply to the students themselves):

1. Endorse, support, or oppose any candidate or nominee for public office or any elected or appointed official regardless of whether such official is a member of the local, state, or federal government;

2. Endorse, support, or oppose any pending or proposed legislation or regulation regardless of whether such legislation or regulation is pending, proposed, or has been enacted at the local, state, or federal level;

3. Endorse, support, or oppose any pending or proposed court litigation regardless of whether such court case or judicial action is at the local, state, or federal level;

4. Advocate one side of a social, political, or cultural issue that is a matter of partisan controversy;

5. Endorse, support, or engage in any activities that hamper

or impede the lawful access of military recruiters to campus; and

6. Endorse, support, or engage in any activities that hamper or impede the actions of state, local, or federal law enforcement.

The regulations promulgated pursuant to this act shall apply to all teachers at public educational institutions, tenured and non-tenured. Moreover, the regulations shall contain clear guidelines for enforcement and provide penalties for violations, up to and including termination. The state's [board of education or other relevant regulating body] shall provide written notification to all teachers, parents, and students of their respective rights and responsibilities under the regulations promulgated pursuant to this act and shall provide at least three hours of annual continuing teacher education instruction to teachers to instruct them regarding their responsibilities under said regulations.

Moreover, we call on the state's professional teacher organizations and unions to voluntarily adopt an educators' code of ethics and professional responsibility that incorporates the above principles and specifically prohibits teachers in K–12 schools from using the classroom for political indoctrination.

Acknowledgments

I would like to acknowledge the support of Ron Robinson and the Young America's Foundation, which made possible many of my speaking engagements on college campuses when student governments would not fund them, and the Intercollegiate Studies Institute for the same reason. I am grateful to Stephen Balch, who has provided invaluable advice in the academic freedom campaign; to Ryan Call, who helped launch the academic freedom campaign; to David French, who crafted the K-12 Academic Bill of Rights; to Stanley Fish, who has been an able critic and prompted me to make amendments to this text; to my campaign staff, Sara Dogan and Brad Shipp; to Jacob Laksin, a fine young writer for *Frontpagemag.com,* who has provided point-by-point rebuttals of the opposition; to Sol Stern for his pioneering work on social justice education; to Gib Armstrong for sponsoring the legislation that made the Pennsylvania Academic Freedom Hearings possible; to Stephen Miller, head of the Duke chapter of Students for Academic Freedom, who organized the Duke event; to my executive assistant, Elizabeth Ruiz, who went over the manuscript and helped track down the footnotes; and to my longtime partner and cherished friend Peter Collier, who has watched my back and helped with this book as he has with so many others.

Notes

Preface to the Paperback Edition

[1] Stephen H. Aby, editor, *The Academic Bill of Rights,* 2007, p. 1.

[2] Aby, op. cit., p. 197. See pp. 39–45 of the present text for a discussion of Joan Wallach Scott

[3] Ibid.

[4] John K. Wilson, *Patriotic Correctness,* 2008, p. 70

[5] Bruce L.R. Smith, Jeremy D. Mayer, L. D. Fritschler, *Closed Minds? Politics and Ideology in American Universities,* Brookings, 2008

[6] *Closed Minds,* op. cit. p. 96

[7] The legislation which I am associated with can be found here: http://www.studentsforacademicfreedom.org/documents/?c=Legislation-Texts.

[8] Pp. 17–18; 71–80

[9] Confusion on this matter has arisen because most universities do provide grievance machinery for students who feel they have been unfairly graded. Administrators who testified at the Pennsylvania hearings played on this confusion to claim that their students' academic freedom was already protected and did not require an Academic Bill of Rights. But the matter of grading is only one area affecting the academic freedom of students. The templates for the existing grievance procedures do not include statements defining academic freedom and consequently do not provide guidelines to students, or a framework for academic freedom complaints. One of the issues brought before the Pennsylvania hearings was that students were unaware of the academic freedom statements of their universities (which at the time did not apply to students) and therefore would be unaware of any rights they might have under them. One of the Committee recommendations was to make students aware of their rights.

[10] http://www.nytimes.com/2005/12/25/national/25bias.html?_r=1&scp=2&sq=gibson%20armstrong&st=cse&oref=slogin; David Horowitz, Ideologues at the Lectern, *Los Angeles Times,* January 23, 2006 http://www.frontpagemag.com/Articles/Read.aspx?GUID=906B5004-A8A5-4B7A-8927-35F806E5BE41.

[11] *Indoctrination U.,* pp. 17-18

[12] *Closed Minds,* op. cit., pp. 129-133

[13] *Indoctrination U.,* op. cit. p. 80. In fact, the hearings were designed to be as far from a McCarthy witch-hunt as possible. They specifically excluded the mention of any professors' or students' names, precisely to avoid the abuses for which McCarthy was famous. On the first day of the hearings, the Committee chairman, Tom Stevenson laid down the hearings guidelines: "This Committee's focus will be on the [academic] institutions and their policies, not on professors, not on students." The Committee strictly adhered to this directive, which didn't dissuade Curry from making his irresponsible attacks.

[14] Most of this testimony is reprinted in Chapter 4 of *Indoctrination U,* pp. 71–80

[15] This part of my testimony is not included in the present volume, but can be found here: http://www.frontpagemag.com/Articles/Printable.aspx? GUID={093DA6DC-A6C5-4269-86C7-89E28BD8BFA6}.

[16] One of them, Lynn Herman, represented a district containing Penn State University and was retiring from office.

[17] I was the author the original report which was then revised by the majority counsel. It was to be ratified by the Republican caucus a week before the filing date but two Republicans, including Herman, failed to show up, making a quorum impossible. A week later Herman and the Democrats staged their coup. The Republicans, demoralized by their electoral defeat, and facing a majority coalition of the Democrats and the two Republicans, agreed to sign on to the final result, which expressed the position the Democrats had maintained throughout the hearings (that there was no problem and the hearings were essentially a waste of time).

[18] The text of the original report before it was gutted and its recommendations rewritten by the Democrats and Republican legislator Lynn Herman can be found here: http://www.studentsforacademicfreedom.org/news/ 2324/pennsylvanias-academic-freedom-reforms.

[19] Ibid.

[20] Administrators from Penn State, Temple and the University of Pittsburgh all testified, falsely, that students were already protected and that complaints were rare. At Penn State, to take one example, there was indeed an academic freedom policy but it could only be found in the university's "Employee Handbook" and its grievance procedure specifically stated that it was for faculty members. This defect was remedied by the passage of Faculty Senate Resolution 20.00, which was a direct response to the hearings. None of these facts were reported by the education press, and none appear in *Closed Minds.*

[21] *Indoctrination U,* pp. 122–3.

[22] A copy of the complaint was sent to me by Abigail Beardsley.

[23] I advised Mr. Fluehr throughout the process. Mr. Fluehr also filed a complaint about a second class that was rejected. A record of his complaints is available at: http://www.discoverthenetworks.org/viewSubCategory.asp?id=522.

Preface

[1] For a portrait of these academic radicals, see David Horowitz, *The Professors*, 2006.

[2] See Chapter Six below; and Sol Stern, " 'Social Justice' and Other High School Indoctrinations," *Frontpagemagazine.com*, April 13, 2006.

[3] The 160 campus chapters of Students for Academic Freedom are autonomous. For information on this movement see: www.studentsforacademicfreedom.org.

[4] For reasons described in *The Professors*, these activists are almost exclusively on the left.

Chapter 1: Academic Freedom

[1] The complete text of the Academic Bill of Rights is reprinted in the Appendix to this volume. Stephen Balch, president of the National Association of Scholars, made extensive revisions to the original text and played an important role in its wording.

[2] http://www.campus-watch.org/article/id/566.

[3] Ibid. The document was written by two academics, Arthur O. Lovejoy and E. R. A. Seligman.

[4] http://www.aaup.org/Com-a/index.htm. The 1970 statement added the word "persistently" to the 1940 statement: "teachers should be careful not to *persistently* introduce into their teaching controversial matter which has no relation to their subject"—but the intent was the same.

[5] Some examples are provided in Chapter Three below. Others can be found at http://www.studentsforacademicfreedom. org/comp/default.asp; www. noindoctrination.org; and www.ratemyprofessors.com. See also David Horowitz, *The Professors*, 2006.

[6] A third statement was posted by Gary Holcomb, an associate professor of English at Emporia State University:

> Date: 8/16/2006
> From: Gary Holcomb
> I have used Sam Hamill's Poets Against the War (Thunder's Mouth Press/Nation Books, 2003) in a course on Literature and Globalization. With poems by Creeley, Dove, Merwin, Pinsky, Rich, Snodgrass—

almost a who's who of contemporary poets—mixed with works by unknown and less frequently published writers, the book makes a powerful lyrical statement on the Iraq war. And given its dedication to Laura Bush, the instructor has the opportunity to discuss the interchanges between art, politics, and war. The anthology illustrates that an organized cultural front persists in posing dissent against reactionary nationalist forces and the effects of globalization.

[7] Students for Academic Freedom now has chapters on 160 college campuses; see www.studentsforacademicfreedom.org.

[8] http://www.studentsforacademicfreedom.org/archive/2005/June/UUP VoiceBullofRights043005.htm.

[9] http://www.studentsforacademicfreedom.org/reports/FacultyStudies.htm. I began the academic freedom campaigns with an attempt to demonstrate there was a problem, which led to several of these studies.

[10] In my view such disparate representation was not (and could not be) the result of random processes but reflected a politically corrupted hiring process in the form of an informal blacklist, and it was the result of the same trends that had corrupted the academic curriculum and had caused the wave of unprofessional behavior in the classroom. See Horowitz, *The Professors,* 2006.

[11] http://www.ratio.se/pdf/wp/dk_aw_voter.pdf, p. 27. Among instructional staff, the figure may be even higher.

[12] These developments have been the subject of numerous books, including Dinesh D'Souza, *Illiberal Education,* 1992; Roger Kimball, *Tenured Radicals,* 1998; Harvey Silverglate and Alan Kors, *The Shadow University,* 1999; Daphne Patai and Noretta Koertge, *Professing Feminism: Education and Indoctrination in Women's Studies,* 2003; and most comprehensively Neil Hamilton, *Zealotry and Academic Freedom,* 1995.

[13] http://www.studentsforacademicfreedom.org/archive/September2004/VictoryinColoradoDhstory091304.htm.

[14] For example, they showed no concern over violations and no interest in holding hearings to ascertain whether the reforms were actually being implemented.

[15] Information about these meetings was leaked to the press by two individuals I had temporarily hired to assist me who became disgruntled when I replaced them.

[16] Peggy Lowe, "GOP Takes On Leftist Education," *Rocky Mountain News,* September 6, 2003.

[17] The text of the Academic Bill of Rights was readily available to Lowe, as it was to journalists generally, on our website at www.studentsforacademic freedom.org.

[18] *Denver Post* editorial, September 13, 2003.

[19] Press reportage on the academic freedom campaign in Colorado is available at http://www.studentsforacademicfreedom.org/reports/COBattle.html.

[20] Gail Schoettler, "Mind Police Are At It Again," *Denver Post,* September 14, 2005.

[21] I am referring to the systematic decline of faculty with conservative and libertarian views during the last thirty years, which cannot be explained in any other way. I have dealt with this issue and described the methods of exclusion in *The Professors,* chs. 1 and 4.

[22] http://billmon.org/archives/001752.html. The author of this attack, Billmon, has also attacked me in an article he posted on the al-Jazeera website: http://www.aljazeerah.info/Opinion%20editorials/2006%20Opinion%20 Editorials/June/13%20o/God%20and%20Money%20at%20Yale%20Inside%20 History%20of%20the%20Israel%20Lobby%20By%20Bill%20Mon.htm.

[23] Readers are invited to type the words "David Horowitz+McCarthyism" into the Google search engine and see for themselves.

[24] Stanley Fish, "Save the World on Your Own Time," *Chronicle of Higher Education,* January 23, 2003.

[25] Stanley Fish, "Larry Summers, Ward Churchill and Chickens Coming Home to Roost . . .," http://www.studentsforacademicfreedom.org/archive/2005/ October2005/FishChurchillandSummers101705.htm.

[26] http://www.studentsforacademicfreedom.org/archive/2006/July2006/ NYTStanleyFishMeaningofAF072406.htm.

[27] Stanley Fish, "Think Again," *New York Times* online edition, May 2, 2006.

[28] Even the ethnic diversity principle as applied in the academic arena is limited to a few designated groups. I am not in sympathy with ethnic diversity quotas and I certainly am not proposing intellectual diversity quotas. The idea is that there should not be merely one point of view.

[29] *Daily Collegian* (Penn State), April 13, 2006.

[30] http://guru.psu.edu/POLICIES/OHR/hr64.html#A.

[31] Robert Post, "The Structure of Academic Freedom," in *Academic Freedom after September 11,* ed. Beshara Doumani, 2006.

[32] Ibid., p. 69.

[33] Exceptions are made to the Ph.D. requirement, but this is normally done in light of some comparable academic achievement.

[34] Post, "The Structure of Academic Freedom." The term "scholar's profession" is in the 1915 Declaration of Principles.

[35] *Frontpagemag.com,* April 18, 2006.

[36] See Chapter Four in this volume for my testimony at the hearings and Chapter Six for an account of the legislation.

Chapter 2: A Revealing Debate

[1] Barney Keller, "Horowitz Safe Zone Highlights Hypocrisy," *Chicago Maroon,* May 12, 2006. The administration official did not bother to welcome me or even speak to me while I was there.

[2] David Horowitz, *Uncivil Wars: The Controversy over Reparations for Slavery,* 2002, p. 32.

[3] Two such universities were Gonzaga, where an e-mail to this effect was circulated to students by philosophy professor Mark Alfino, and the University of Missouri, where a flyer with similar claims was circulated by biology professor Miriam Golomb. There were others.

[4] My own speeches generally had to be subsidized by the Young America's Foundation and the Intercollegiate Studies Institute.

[5] According to the conservative students who invited me.

[6] This and other quotations from the event are taken from the audio provided by Reed.

[7] Noam Chomsky, *Hegemony or Survival: America's Quest for Global Dominance,* 2004.

[8] Hayek, who is generally regarded as a libertarian, wrote a famous postscript, "Why I Am Not a Conservative," but this shorthand accurately reflects how he is perceived in the academy.

[9] The debate was recorded by Reed. All quotations from the debate are taken from the transcript, which is available at www.studentsforacademicfreedom.org.

[10] To be fair, Steinberger also attacked a one-sentence characterization of a book I had made in an article about Bates University, which I had visited more than seven years earlier.

[11] The pamphlets are included in the essay collections *The Art of Political War and Other Radical Pursuits,* 2000; and *How to Beat the Democrats and Other Radical Ideas,* 2002.

[12] *The Art of Political War,* p. 10.

[13] Ibid., p. 38.

[14] Ibid., p. 11.

[15] Ibid., p. 47.

[16] I maintained a correspondence with Dean Steinberger after the debate and was able to persuade him to address the issues and provide me with a critique of the Academic Bill of Rights. While he conceded no ground either to my critique of the university or to the remedy suggested, it was the most intellectually substantive and intelligent critique that had been written of the bill, and I answered it and published the exchange on my website at http://www.studentsforacademicfreedom.org/reports/HorowitzSteinbergerDebateonAF.htm?id =4e7wgf9fn5ohqsfetzz8hrpmiz4jjevo.

Chapter 3: Facing the Opposition

[1] E.g., Paul Krugman, "An Academic Question," *New York Times,* April 5, 2005.

[2] It was even argued by four social scientists in an academic journal. Cf. http://www.studentsforacademicfreedom.org/archive/2006/January2006/ArtEcksteinPittofAcadBias011206.htm.

[3] http://www.studentsforacademicfreedom.org/reports/Horowitz Steinberger DebateonAF.htm?id=4e7wgf9fn5ohqsfetzz8hrpmiz4jjevo.

[4] http://www.studentsforacademicfreedom.org/archive/2005/October2005/GannettNewsConservGroupSeeks101305.htm.

[5] These responses can be read in the testimonies to the Pennsylvania Committee and in the press files at www.studentsforacademicfreedom.org.

[6] See Chapter Five below.

[7] These were the reactions, for example, to Colorado high school student Sean Allen's taping of a political harangue by his geography teacher, and also the stock responses by professors to the academic freedom hearings in Pennsylvania, as well as to my book.

[8] Graham Larkin, "David Horowitz's War on Rational Discourse," *Inside HigherEd.com,* April 25, 2005. My responses to Larkin's distortions and fabrications can be found at: http://www.studentsforacademicfreedom.org/reports/RepliestoCritics.htm.

[9] As noted earlier, I was referring to the 300-odd ethics charges that proved insubstantial in the end.

[10] David Horowitz, *The Art of Political War,* p. 24.

[11] Ellen Schrecker, "Worse Than McCarthy," *Chronicle of Higher Education,* February 10, 2006, http://chronicle.com/free/v52/i23/23b02001.htm. The article, which appeared in the magazine section, the *Chronicle Review,* also attacked Daniel Pipes and the website *CampusWatch.org.*

[12] For the text of the Academic Bill of Rights see the Appendix to the present volume.

[13] David Horowitz, "In Defense of Intellectual Diversity," *Chronicle of Higher Education,* February 10, 2004.

[14] Ellen Schrecker, *Many Are the Crimes: McCarthyism in America,* 1999, cited in Jacob Laksin, "Ellen Schrecker's McCarthyite Crusade," *Frontpagemag. com,* February 16, 2006.

[15] Ellen Schrecker, *No Ivory Tower: McCarthyism and the Universities,* 1988, cited in Laksin, "Ellen Schrecker's McCarthyite Crusade."

[16] David Horowitz, "Ward Churchill Is Just the Beginning," *Rocky Mountain News,* February 8, 2005.

[17] Scott was the chairman of the committee from 1999 until June 2005, which

spanned the formative years of the conflict. She would have overseen the AAUP's seminal statement condemning the bill.

[18] Transcript, Public Hearing of Select Committee on Academic Freedom in Higher Education, November 9, 2005, p. 187.

[19] My own father, Philip Horowitz, was a member of this union and was fired for refusing to answer questions under the Fineberg Law.

[20] He was tried for daring to suggest that artists should be able to express themselves freely. See Norma Barzman, *The Red and the Blacklist: Memoir of a Hollywood Insider,* 2003.

[21] Bella V. Dodd, *School of Darkness,* 1954.

[22] It is becoming fashionable on the left to describe this kind of treason as not really treason by claiming that American Communists "transcended the nationalist meta-narrative"; or, as Ellen Shrecker declared when she could no longer deny the enormous scale of Communist spying for the Soviet Union, that American Communists "practiced a different kind of patriotism."

[23] Joan W. Scott, "Academic Freedom As an Ethical Practice," in *The Future of Academic Freedom,* ed. Louis Menand, 1996.

[24] In fact, as the result of a Supreme Court ruling, the pensions of all the teachers fired were restored with interest a decade later. Scott's silence on this point is simply more prevarication.

[25] Joan Wallach Scott, *Gender and the Politics of History,* 1999, Introduction.

[26] http://www.militantislammonitor.org/article/id/1927: *New York Times,* April 18, 2006.

[27] "Joan Wallach Scott on Threats to Academic Freedom," http://www.aaup.org/publications/Academe/2005/05so/05soscot.htm.

[28] http://wrmea.com/archives/December_2005/0512046.html; Jane Adas, "Princeton Panelists Share Cautionary Tales of Dangers to Academic Freedom," *Washington Report on Middle East Affairs,* December 2005.

[29] The conference was intended, as Scott also asserted, to give a new public forum to advocates of boycotting Israeli scholars. See her comments in the *InsideHigherEd.com* Comments section for February 9, 2006: http://www.insidehighered.com/news/2006/02/09/aaup. See also Cary Nelson's information in the same Comments section, but later, on February 10, 2006. Nelson, who was subsequently elected president of the AAUP, was outraged to discover this. In May 2006, radical factions within the British union of teachers of higher education did in fact attempt to reignite the boycott of Israeli scholars: see *InsideHigherEd.com* for May 12, 2006.

[30] http://www.aaup.org/statements/SpchState/Statements/BillofRights.htm. For a reply to the AAUP's statement, see http://www.studentsforacademic freedom.org/archive/december/HorowitzAAUPResponse120503.htm.

[31] E.g., "'Blacklisted' UT Professor Visits Hilltop" was the headline in a story by Ashley Jorgensen in the Southern Methodist University campus paper about a talk given by Robert Jensen, one of the academics profiled in my book *The Professors* (*SMUDailyCampus.com,* April 26, 2006). Needless to say, I hadn't recommended that Jensen be fired for his views or that anyone holding such views should not be hired, a fact that Jensen himself admitted in his speech: "'David Horowitz is not arguing to eliminate people with certain beliefs, but he is arguing that there needs to be a balance of opinion,' he said." Actually, I have never even called for "balance," only that there should be a pluralism of views represented on a faculty.

[32] http://www.centredaily.com/mld/centredaily/news/opinion/14359363.htm?template=contentModules/printstory.jsp.

Chapter 4: Indoctrination U.

[1] For an archive of studies of indoctrination curricula in American universities, see http://www.discoverthenetworks.org/viewSubCategory.asp?id=522.

[2] http://csf.colorado.edu/gimenez/soc.5055/index.html.

[3] http://feministstudies.ucsc.edu/resCareers.html.

[4] http://feministstudies.ucsc.edu/resMajor.html.

[5] Compare this with the Sproul clause quoted as an epigraph to this text.

[6] Several of these programs are examined here: http://www.discoverthenetworks.org/groupProfile.asp?grpid=6680: cf. also http://www.discoverthenetworks.org/groupProfile.asp?grpid=6680.

[7] For the text of the letter, cf. http://www.studentsforacademicfreedom.org/literature/CSPC_BallState.pdf.

[8] David P. Barash and Charles P. Webel, *Peace and Conflict Studies* (Sage Publications, 2002), p. x.

[9] Ibid., p. 498.

[10] Ibid., p. 499.

[11] Ibid., pp. 14–15.

[12] Ibid., p. 80.

[13] Ibid., pp. 80–81.

[14] Ibid., p. 81.

[15] Ibid.

[16] http://uts.cc.utexas.edu/~dcloud/Politics2.html.

[17] http://www.internationalsocialist.org/what_we_stand_for.html.

[18] http://uts.cc.utexas.edu/~dcloud/socialchangesyll.htm. The entire syllabus for the course is available at this site.

[19] Ibid.

[20] This section is based on testimony presented to the Appropriations Committee of the Kansas House of Representatives on March 15, 2006.

[21] Kansas Board of Regents Policy Statement on the Use of Controversial Material in Instruction, Including the Use of Sexually Explicit Materials in Instruction (adopted April 23, 2004), http://www.provost.ku.edu/policy/controversial_material/controversial_%20material_policy_042304.doc.

[22] This clause is identical to the "1940 Statement of Principles on Academic Freedom and Tenure" of the American Association of University Professors.

[23] I owe this example to Stanley Fish.

[24] http://www.k-state.edu/womst/.

[25] Two other points, which can be ambiguously interpreted, have been dropped for concision.

[26] http://www.ku.edu/~wsku/.

[27] http://www.utexas.edu/courses/arens/wgs1/wgs1syll.html.

[28] One important and book-length study of this problem is *Professing Feminism: Education and Indoctrination in Women's Studies,* 2003, by the above-mentioned Daphne Patai and Noretta Koertge.

[29] http://www.k-state.edu/socialwork/main.html.

[30] http://www.k-state.edu/socialwork/socwk525.htm.

[31] http://www.k-state.edu/socialwork/socwk510.htm.

[32] Phyllis J. Day, *A New History of Social Welfare,* 5th ed., 2005. According to the notice on Amazon.com, the fifth edition of this book includes "major emphasis on the Afro-centric paradigm." On the fraudulent racism of the Afrocentric paradigm, see the discussion below.

[33] Phyllis J. Day, *A New History of Social Welfare,* 4th ed., 2003, p. 17.

[34] Ibid., p. 455.

[35] With the exception of the passage on the African American Studies Department at Temple, the text that follows is an edited version of my testimony before the Select Committee on Academic Freedom in Higher Education of the Pennsylvania House of Representatives held on January 10, 2006. Other testimony is available at: http://www.studentsforacademicfreedom.org/actions (boxattop)/Pennsylvaniapage/PennHearings.htm.

[36] As noted, I have personally interviewed hundreds of students who have been in classes in which their professors have made speeches against President Bush or the war in Iraq, for example, in courses that were not about George Bush or the war in Iraq. I have spoken at Penn State (twice), Lehigh University, the University of Pennsylvania, Swarthmore (twice), Duquesne Law and other Pennsylvania schools.

[37] Several of the legislators asked the president of Temple, when he testified, how many complaints he had received from students about problems like this, and whether there were in fact any such complaints. Temple's president couldn't think of one. I ask readers to consider: if they were a history major at

Temple and also a Republican, and went to the office of their adviser, who happened to be the chairman of the history department, and heard him say in a totally inappropriate context that if George Bush were re-elected America would become a fascist state, and saw on every one of their professors' office doors an "Elect John Kerry" sign, would they complain publicly about these facts? Would they decide to go over the heads of their professor and adviser to a dean or provost to complain about this harassment? My guess is that like most students, the reader would decide to grin and bear the whole experience and get on with their academic career.

[38] These points were made by Stephen Balch, president of the National Association of Scholars, at an earlier hearings session.

[39] Transcript, Public Hearing of Select Committee on Academic Freedom in Higher Education, November 9, 2005, p. 111.

[40] The "1940 Statement of Principles on Academic Freedom and Tenure" of the American Association of University Professors.

[41] The "1940 Statement" is written into the faculty union contract with the Pennsylvania State System of Higher Education, http://www.passhe.edu/content/?/administration/HR/labor/unions/apscuf&item=13460, pp. 3–4.

[42] www.studentsforacademicfreedom.org.

[43] http://courses.temple.edu/ih/ihtest/ih52/revolution/marx/marx_facpersp.htm.

[44] *Gendered Voices: Selected Readings from the American Experience,* ed. Keith Gumery; *Exploring Language,* ed. Gary Goshgarian; *Great Divides: Readings in Social Inequality in the United States,* ed. Thomas M. Shapiro; and *Writing Lives: Exploring Literacy and Community,* ed. Garnes, et al.

[45] In addition, the words "Abyssinia Ancient City" were changed in the example to "Mesopotamia," but otherwise the text is identical to the text in the Temple catalogue. The spelling of "Afrikan American Studies" is as it appears in the course description rather than in the official departmental description. http://astro.temple.edu/~karanja/aas051syllsp03.pdf#search='the%20reading%20materials%20are%20our%20map%2C%20and%20Afrikan%20consciousness%20is%20our%20guide.%20Let%20us%20continue%20the%20process%20of%20Afrikan%20liberation%21%E2%80%9D.'

[46] Mary Lefkowitz, *Not Out of Africa: How Afrocentrism Became an Excuse to Teach Myths As History,* 1996.

[47] http://www.studentsforacademicfreedom.org/archive/2005/October2005/DavidFrenchPAacadfreehearingstestimony102805.htm; and *University Times,* November 23, 2005, http://www.umc.pitt.edu:591/u/FMPro?-db=ustory&-lay=a&-format=d.html&storyid=4172&-Find.

[48] "Good Night, Good Luck," *Centre Daily Times,* November 30, 2005.

Chapter 5: Dangerous Professors

[1] Thus the *Chronicle of Higher Education* interviewed one of the subjects of the book, Professor Michael Berube, asking him, "What makes you so dangerous?" Berube's answer: "My slap shot." This was typical of the academic left's effort—an effort that included the *Chronicle,* which never reviewed the book—to dispose of the serious questions it raised by trivializing them. Jennifer Jacobson, "Dangerous Minds," *Chronicle of Higher Education,* February 17, 2006.

[2] These included the American Historical Association, the Modern Language Association, the American Anthropological Association, the American Philosophical Association, the American Library Association and of course the American Association of University Professors.

[3] For samples, see the articles on, and responses of, professors Caroline Higgins and David Barash posted at www.dangerousprofessors.com.

[4] http://dangerousprofessors.net/2006/08/reply-to-critic-attack-of-academic.html.

[5] Many of these attacks and my responses can be found at www.dangprofs.com.

[6] http://www.freeexchangeoncampus.org/index.php?option=com_docman&task=down&bid=26. Actually, there were 101, if one counted the profile of Ward Churchill that I had drawn in the book's introduction; or 102 if one included the portrait of Cornel West in an analytic chapter near the end.

[7] These include the American Federation of Teachers, the American Association of University Professors, the Soros-funded university operation called Campus Progress, the American Civil Liberties Union, People for the American Way, U.S. PIRG and the Center for Free Speech on Campus, another union front. http://www.freeexchangeoncampus.org/.

[8] http://www.insidehighered.com/news/2006/05/09/report.

[9] A comprehensive, point-by-point refutation of "Facts Count" is available at http://www.studentsforacademicfreedom.org/reports/FreeExchange RebuttalPage.htm. This response was written by Jacob Laksin, who summarizes: "Much of the Free Exchange report is based on grievances voiced by . . . professors [profiled in the text], whose charges against the book the Free Exchange authors accept uncritically. Every one of these charges is answered in the present response. Some of the individuals, like Richard Falk, Larry Estrada and Gordon Fellman, misrepresent their past statements and writings. Others, like Matthew Evangelista, Mari Matsuda and Elizabeth Brumfiel, offer disingenuous accounts of their past (and ongoing) role in the continued politicization of American universities. Two professors, Marc Becker and Sam Richards, even attempt to disguise their expressed support for politics in the classroom by posing as champions of intellectual diversity and—in Becker's case—non-ideological teaching. Not one of the professors mentioned in the

Free Exchange report appears willing to openly defend the partisan politics and political extremism that flourish in the university curriculum or to frankly acknowledge their role in promoting these developments. This bad faith permeates the report 'Facts Count' and renders its title ironic indeed."

[10] Horowitz, *The Professors,* p. xxvi.

[11] Ibid., ch. 3.

[12] Ibid., ch. 4: "The Representative Nature of the Professors Profiled in this Text." In the text I scaled down the estimate by half to be "conservative," but in the absence of further investigations to the contrary there is probably no need for such caution.

[13] When I was at Columbia College in the 1950s, for example, there was a reluctance to look at events more recent than twenty-five years in the past because of the dangers of "present-mindedness" and the fear that events so fresh could not be examined with "scholarly disinterest."

[14] Neal Sen Gupta, "Audience Members, T-Shirts Blast Speaker's Views," *Duke Chronicle,* March 9, 2006, http://www.dukechronicle.com/media/storage/paper884/news/2006/03/08/News/Audience.Members.TShirts.Blast.Speakers.Views1659278.shtml?norewrite200605101814&sourcedomain=www.dukechronicle.com.

[15] I have edited the speech for this text.

[16] Among those refusing to invite me were the departments of Anthropology, Women's Studies, African and African American Studies, Literature, Philosophy, English, the Multicultural Center, the Major Speakers Program, the Institute of U.S. Critical Studies, and the John Hope Franklin Center. All were approached by Stephen Miller, the student who organized my event.

[17] Among those that did agree to sponsor the event, which was principally underwritten by the Young America's Foundation, a conservative institution, were the Office of the Provost, the Terry Sanford Institute, and Duke Student Government and Student Affairs.

[18] Subsequent to this speech, al-Arian pled guilty to conspiracy to providing material support to a terrorist organization, including deceiving the U.S. government about the terrorist political connections of men seeking visas to the U.S., and was sentenced to deportation after a period in prison.

[19] *Raleigh-Durham News and Observer,* March 7, 2006.

Chapter 6: Battle Lines

[1] Scheuerman is also head of United University Professions, an organization that bills itself as the "nation's largest higher education union," representing 30,000 employees on 29 campuses of the State University of New York.

[2] *UUP Voice,* April 2005.

[3] Ibid.

[4] http://www.insidehighered.com/layout/set/print/news/2005/04/18/aft.

[5] See, for example, the many commentaries by myself and Sara Dogan, national campus director of Students for Academic Freedom, at www.studentsfor academicfreedom.org.

[6] http://www.studentsforacademicfreedom.org/reports/ACEStatementPage. htm?id=4e7wgf9fn5ohqsfetzz8hrpmiz4jjevo: author's conversation with Terry Hartle, vice president for government affairs of the American Council on Education.

[7] http://www.goacta.org/publications/Reports/IntellectualDiversityFinal.pdf.

[8] Scott Jaschik, "Tactical Shift or Tactical Error?" *InsideHigherEd.com,* October 3, 2005.

[9] A transcript of the entire conference is available at http://www.discover thenetworks.org/viewSubCategory.asp?id=349.

[10] http://www.studentsforacademicfreedom.org/archive/2005/October2005/ GannettNewsConservGroupSeeks101305.htm.

[11] http://www.frontpagemag.com/Articles/Printable.asp?ID=22004.

[12] Ibid.

[13] http://uupinfo.org/voice/apr/06/0406p2.pdf.

[14] A transcript of Bennish's remarks is available at http://www.psaf.org/ archive/2006/March2006/BennishTranscript032806.html.

[15] I am indebted to Sol Stern for his pioneering work in identifying and describing the social justice movement in K–12 education. Cf. http://www. city-journal.org/html/16_3_ed_school.html.

[16] Eric Gutstein, *Reading and Writing the World with Mathematics,* Routledge, 2006, pp. 1–2.

[17] Ibid., pp. 140–41. Gutstein contrasts this to "biased teaching," the difference being that biased teaching is indoctrination that conceals the fact that other points of view exist, while partisan teaching presents other points of view in order to refute them.

[18] Ibid., p. xiv. The editor of the series is Michael W. Apple, the John Bascom Professor of Curriculum and Instruction and Educational Policy Studies at the University of Wisconsin, Madison.

[19] See profile of William Ayers in Horowitz, *The Professors,* 2006.

[20] These efforts include antimilitary recruitment drives at high schools; incitements to U.S. soldiers stationed in Iraq to become "conscientious objectors"; and breaking into congressional hearings where U.S. officials are testifying, as a "protest" against the war.

Coda: Academic Progress

[1] Out-of-state students pay $30,000 a year to attend the University of Colorado. There were more than a thousand cancellations, of which 40 percent were out-of-state.

[2] "Report of the Investigative Committee of the Standing Committee on Research Misconduct at the University of Colorado at Boulder concerning Allegations of Academic Misconduct against Professor Ward Churchill," May 9, 2006, http://www.colorado.edu/news/reports/churchill/churchillreport051606.html.

[3] Ibid., p. 101.

[4] http://www.rockymountainnews.com/drmn/local/article/0,1299,DRMN_15_4771570,00.html.

[5] "Report of the Investigative Committee," p. 98.

[6] Ibid.

[7] Ibid., p. 21.

[8] Ibid., p. 4.

[9] Ibid., p. 98.

[10] Michael Berube, *What's Liberal about the Liberal Arts: Classroom Politics and "Bias" in Higher Education*, 2006, p. 29.

[11] Ibid., pp. 30–31.

[12] Ibid., p. 33.

[13] Ibid., p. 34.

[14] E.g., cf. *MediaMatters*, "*Hannity & Colmes:* Horowitz Ignored Facts Undermining GOP Student's Claim That Professor Failed Him for 'Pro-American' Paper," February 22, 2005; also www.outsidethebeltway.com/archives/8841; and www.poliblogger.com/index.php?p=5923.

[15] Ahmad al-Qloushi, "Dissident Arab Gets the Treatment," *Frontpagemag.com*, January 6, 2005.

[16] Michael Wiesner, "Collegiate Intimidation," *Frontpagemag.com*, December 15, 2004.

[17] Allan Bloom, *The Closing of the American Mind*, 1987, p. 324.

[18] http//www:cms.studentsforacademicfreedom.org/index.php?option=com_content&task=view&id=2324&itemid=40.

[19] http://www.psu.edu/ufs/policies/20-00.htm.

[20] The Temple policy is available at: http://policies.temple.edu/getdoc.asp?policy_no=03.70.02: cf. also http://www.studentsforacademicfreedom.org/archive/2006/July2006/TempleTrusteesAdoptPolicyPressRelease072106.htm.

[21] Valerie Richardson, "Academic Manifesto Takes Root," *Washington Times*, July 3, 2006. The AFT official is Jamie Horwitz.

Appendices

[1] This is a modified version of Princeton's mission statement, as quoted in Alan Kors and Harvey Silverglate, *The Shadow University,* 1998, p. 62.

[2] Ibid., p. 50.

Index